BANANA REPUBLIC UK?

Vote Rigging, Fraud and Error in

British Elections Since 2001

Sam Buckley

The author would like to thank the Open Rights Group for their kind permission to quote extensively from their reports.

This book is dedicated to my marvellous partner, Sally Dwelly and my wonderful parents John and Janet Buckley, without whose cries of "Get out of your pit and go and do something useful!" it would undoubtedly never have been written. Thanks are due to the officials and researchers who answered my questions. It goes without saying that any errors are my own. Lastly, this book is dedicated to the five Hastings CSA union officers sacked for fighting against injustice.

CONTENTS

Preface   5

What Is Democracy   8

The Mechanics of Voting and Vote Rigging   11

Birmingham 2004   18

European Elections 2004   42

Incidents In The General Election of 2005   46

Am I My Brother's Cheater? vote rigging

in internal party elections   60

Evoting, Ecounting, EDS and other tales of

an ordinary madness   76

One Step Forward? The Electoral Administration

Act of 2006   91

A Spectre Is Haunting Slough – Ghost voters and
election rigging   97

The Whole World Is Watching   120

The Light At The End of the Tunnel Might Not Be A
Train Coming In the Other Direction: The Political
Parties and Elections Act of 2009   130

The Sealed Ballot Box That Wasn't   132

E counting On Trial – The GLA elections of 2008
and the Scottish Elections of May 2007   134

Glengarry, Glenrothes   144

Night of the Long Lines: The 2010 General Election   147

What Is To Be Done? (To Coin A Phrase)   162

Bibliography and Sources   165

PREFACE

This book is about a subject I believe to be hugely important – ballot rigging in modern Britain. The practice is real and it is widespread. Vote rigging has occurred and been proven to occur in Birmingham, Slough, Peterborough, Reading, Bristol, Burnley, Blackburn, Halton, Guildford, Havant, Bradford and other towns and cities. Election Commissioner Mawrey concluded that the 2004 Birmingham City Council elections "would disgrace a banana republic." In the course of that election there was a small riot as activists from the local Labour party fought to steal postal ballot papers from both the postal workers on their delivery rounds and Labour's rivals from a local Kashmiri party.

A few months before the last General Election (14/01/2010) the Electoral Commission issued a warning that election administrators should be on the alert for fraud or malpractice in the 2010 General Election and local elections as possible narrow margins of victory give rise to the temptation for activists to cheat, or accuse others of cheating. The report also highlights that specialist squads will be operating in all police forces to deal with these allegations. (Guardian 14/01/2010) The Government's Chief Whip responded to a report from the Electoral Commission showing that nearly half of all constituencies did not plan to count the General Election votes overnight by saying "The reason the votes are counted immediately after the polls close is to stop people cheating. Leaving blank ballot papers and lists of those who haven't voted and the ballot boxes all together in the same place overnight is not a reassuring prospect. The scope for fraud is obvious." (Newcastle Journal 13/01/2010). Unfortunately his comments did not get the publicity they deserved possibly because he chose to link them to a bitter attack on the Liberal Democrats in his home city of Newcastle.

Many will point out that ballot rigging, which, so far, has only happened on a large scale in European and local elections where turnouts are usually low and votes often cast purely as a protest, is only one, and arguably not the most important of the flaws in our democracy.

5

After all, doesn't the fact that a newspaper proprietor who may not even have a vote himself has more influence over our rulers than any rank and file voter outside a key marginal make our votes a mockery anyway? Is there a point in voting at all when the main parties – which is to say the only ones with any short term hope of forming a government – share a near identical set of assumptions about the world, so much so that policy advisers frequently flit from one side to the other with little public comment or concern and are quite prepared to break their manifesto promises and their given word?

What about the world of work, where your democratic rights to disagree with your manager are, in practice, whatever laws may say, limited at best?

A particularly blatant example occurred in 2008 when a civil servant working in Hastings applied for and was given permission to stand for the neo-fascist British National Party in local elections despite the protests of the union, who pointed out that the BNP's declared policies were hardly in line with a staff Code of Conduct which stated that workers had a duty to promote diversity in the communities in which they lived and worked. Fair enough, you may say, the BNP is a legal party after all whatever anyone thinks of it. The sting in the tail however is that a few days later members of the Public and Commercial Services union handing out anti-fascist leaflets were ordered to stop by a senior manager, part of the same Area management team that had given the BNP member permission to stand, on the grounds that as civil servants *they were obliged to be politically neutral!* (Morning Star 29 April 2008)

Doesn't our voting system, which systematically excludes minority opinion from the legislative chambers, offer a greater cause for concern than fiddled council votes in Burnley or Bradford? And what about basic liberties? After all, as Ignazio Silone said, democracy is not simply universal suffrage, it is "universal suffrage plus certain conditions...equality of rights before the law; liberty...political equality and..freedom of speech" (School for Dictators pp 263).

Britain is now a country where publically naming those killed in an ongoing war (Maya Evans, Naming the Dead) can get you arrested under the Serious Organised Crime Act. It is a country where heckling a government minister whilst attending a conference which that minister is supposedly accountable to can get you arrested under anti terror legislation (Taking Liberties). Bizarrely, it is even a country where on duty police officers will occasionally take time to call on you to voice their disapproval of your opinions *even though they accept that you haven't actually committed a crime.* (Littlejohn's Britain)

The answer is two-fold. Yes, all these points and many more are excellent ones, but they are points that a great many people are aware of and devote their time to trying to publicise. Organised vote rigging however is the subject of occasional newspaper articles, no national campaign and not one book so far, barring the verdict of the 2004 Birmingham election court, despite the facts being available and in the public domain.

Secondly, voting is one of the very few means available to us to attempt to rectify the other flaws in our system and the one that most campaigns advocate. If we let a free and fairly counted system of balloting slip from our hands as so many of our other rights have done or are doing we are left with the options of general strike, armed force or a combination of both. I will declare an interest here; I am an increasingly poor shot at distances much over fifty yards and am allergic to having my head blown off.

That said, countries where there is no peaceful means to effect change invariably become subject to internal violence, that is as close to a law of nature as anything in politics can get.

It is my hope that this book will stimulate wider interest in the subject and, more importantly, inspire people to do something about it.

What Is Democracy ?

Democracy is a Greek word meaning "rule of the people", the *demos* , and it is among the Greek city states that by far the best known and most closely studied examples of any kind of popular rule before the modern era are found.

It is worth noting that the rich and powerful had serious reservations about democracy from the start. "When the poor rule, that is a democracy" wrote Aristotle (pp 39 The Collapse of Democracy") and he did not mean this as a compliment. Plato believed the ideal system to be, not a democracy but rule by an elite of (surprise, surprise) philosophers. Philosophers, being largely drawn from the landed classes that feared untrammelled popular rule would lead to the confiscation of their property, were distinctly suspicious of democracy. The feeling was mutual – it was a democracy that killed Socrates. Nowadays elites tend to pay at least lip service to the democratic idea.

It is also worth noting that the Greeks of the Classical era wouldn't have recognised our system as a democracy at all. The Athenians had directly elected officials as well as some chosen by lot but they were accountable to the Assembly, where any free citizen could stand up and say his piece and which could and did exile or execute those who tried to go against it. As far as it went it was far more democratic than any country today – the catch, of course, was in the words "free citizen". Women had no vote and neither did slaves despite the fact that without women or slaves Athens would have rapidly ceased to exist. Our system they would have recognised as a system of competing oligarchies chosen by democratic input and partially balanced by an unelected chamber and, of course, a monarch, whose powers remain considerable, even though or perhaps because they have largely slipped into the hands of the Parliamentary executive. This is one reason why the Conservative politician Lord Hailsham famously said that Britain was not a democracy, but an "elective dictatorship" (For a hilarious example of how the ancient Athenians might have seen us I recommend "Alexander At The World's End" by Tom Holt)

Our political system then contains only one officially acknowledged powerful democratic element – our power to vote and to vote secretly and as we choose. We have had this power for far less time than many people realise. Prior to 1872 when the Parliamentary and Municipal Elections Act was passed all voting was public. This meant that unless you wielded considerable power and influence in your own right candidates and their supporters could bribe you, kidnap you, threaten you, evict you, sack you, boycott your business or simply hit you repeatedly over the head until you lost all interest in politics. Every one of these methods was repeatedly used over the years. In elections in Kent in the 1830s radical Sir William Courtenay (who was to end his life shot dead by soldiers while leading an abortive labourers' revolt) almost swung the poll in Canterbury with the help of a determined mob but was beaten at his own game in the elections for the county seat where the Tory candidate arrived with a five hundred strong bodyguard equipped with heavy sticks (Battle of Bossenden Wood).

It was not until Gladstone's time that a politician came to power who was not only clear headed enough to see that employees, tenants and small tradesmen would never be politically free while men who had the power to deprive them of their livelihoods could see which way they voted, but willing and able to do something about it.

Almost as a side issue the secret ballot put an end to direct bribery as well , no one being willing to buy a vote without a guarantee that they would get it.

Universal male suffrage didn't arrive until 1918, universal female suffrage until 1928 and businessmen could have several votes until 1948 on the UK mainland. Multiple votes for businessmen lasted for many years longer in Northern Ireland and the struggle for one person one vote there could and has filled books many times the length of this one.

Leaving Northern Ireland aside then we have had universal and equal voting rights in the UK for 61 years at the time of writing – less than a lifetime. As I hope to show, if we do not wake up those votes could be made worthless in a lot less than 61 years.

The Mechanics of Voting and Vote Rigging

Prior to the advent of New Labour in 1997 the details of a British election hadn't changed for at least fifty years. In many respects they still appear the same in most places. Go to a polling station and you will pass a small group seated outside who will ask you for your polling number. There is no reason to give it if you don't want to and many people don't.

These "tellers" are collecting polling numbers for the political parties to which they belong – they have no official status although unofficially they play an important role. The tellers are doing this so that voter numbers can be taken to local party HQ where election agents, frenziedly scanning their canvas returns, can despatch their troops to rout out those of their supporters that haven't come out to vote yet .

They *will* only drag out their own supporters – faced with evidence that the other side haven't stirred election agents and candidates will breathe a huge sigh of relief and let sleeping dogs lie. This is why party canvassers come knocking on your door for weeks before elections (at least if you live in the increasingly rare areas that are both marginal enough to be worth canvassing and where the parties have enough active members to do it.) Canvassers are not, for the most part, trying to win you over, they just want to know who is already on their side so they don't knock on the wrong doors on election day.

The pads tellers use are called Mikardo pads, or Reading pads because they were invented by the Labour MP Ian Mikardo in a determined attempt to hold on to his marginal seat in Reading – an attempt that was successful for many years until he was finally overwhelmed by boundary changes.

Inside the polling station the voter will see two people, a Presiding Officer and a poll clerk seated at a table with a heavily thumbed copy of the Electoral Register and a large metal box with a slit in the top, painted black. If he has his polling card she will give it to one of the two officials, if not they will look up his address, cross it off and hand over a ballot paper. The register they do this on is called the marked register and is retained so that the number of ballot papers issued can be checked to match the number that come out of the box. The voter takes his or her ballot paper into a wooden booth, like a tall three sided box and marks a cross by the candidate of their choice with an old fashioned soft lead pencil before folding the ballot paper and carefully placing it in the ballot box. The voting is done for another year.

Come the close of poll it is the responsibility of the poll clerk and presiding officer to complete their declarations, place the marked register in with the votes ,close the slot at the top of the ballot box, tie it into place and seal the strings with the aid of a heavy, old fashioned stick of sealing wax – one of the very few things sealing wax is still used for. It is then their responsibility to deliver it to the town hall, or wherever the count is taking place and leave it in the custody of the returning officer, seals still unbroken.

It will only be unsealed in the presence of the scrutineers – members of all the parties standing whose first duty it will be to raise Cain in the event of a tampered ballot box being delivered.

The first count will take no account of who votes have been cast for – it is purely to establish that the number of votes in the ballot box matches the number of ballot papers issued. After this votes will be counted under the ferocious scrutiny of party observers who will leap in if they see any of their candidate's votes going into the wrong pile.

In cases where the voter has not put an X beside the candidate of their choice candidates and returning officers will be called over – usually the voter's intention is clear, a tick or a 1 replacing the traditional x – if not debate may rage but everyone involved has good reason for being sensible – their own candidate's votes may be the next to be challenged. If no clear intention can be established the vote will go into the "spoiled ballots" pile.

Eventually, God willing, and possibly after a number of recounts a clear winner will emerge. (On a few occasions an identical number of votes have been cast for the two lead candidates and this has led to elections being, quite literally, decided by the toss of a coin.) Once the returning officer has announced a candidate's election then even if they subsequently realise they read out the wrong name

the candidate is in, pending court action – this is very rare but an example will come up later in this book.

And that is a traditional British election, done and dusted!

A few things will be immediately obvious – at any point it would be extremely hard to cheat. The presiding officer and poll clerk of a polling station may only have met on the day of the election – it would take a considerable feat of organisation and a number of insiders in the local authority to suborn even a significant minority of them and the legal penalties if detected are fierce.

If it could be done, ballot stuffing or the removal of opposition ballots by poll staff is still virtually impossible given that there can be no more or fewer votes inside the box when opened than were issued. Ones best hope would be to "spoil" opposition votes but even there it would become rapidly obvious to the scrutineers and counters if the votes of a particular party in from one polling district were disproportionately *not* spoiled – obvious enough to raise very difficult questions for the poll clerk and presiding officer who have both signed a declaration that the box was sealed at close of poll and never out of their sight at any time during the day until they handed it over to the returning officer.

Secondly, the mere fact that voting is done by pencilling a cross on a piece of paper makes it very hard to interfere with. Unlike the voting machinery used in some countries a pencil will not undervote, will not place an X in the wrong place of its own accord and will not fail to write without it being obvious.

Unlike many countries with more technologically advanced systems, including much of the USA , a recount in a UK election can be instantly and easily performed. It cannot be altered by a computer "glitch", accidental or otherwise and in the event of dispute there is a clear paper trail. Short of having almost everyone involved in the election process paid off (and the sheer *risk* of even *trying* to do that would be enormous) there are only two ways in which an election like this could be properly rigged.

One is by the force of intimidation – having heavies come into the polling booth and look over people's shoulders or a crowd of thugs outside chasing off anyone who they think might be an opposition supporter.

The slightest attempt to do either of these would have the poll clerk and presiding officer calling out the police and halting further proceedings until voting could proceed without fear – something they have both the right and the legal duty to do – even canvassing in the approaches to a polling station is strictly forbidden , the tellers at the door aren't allowed to so much as wear their party rosettes for fear of putting undue pressure on the voting public.

Certainly it could be done if a fundamentally anti-democratic party already controlled the state apparatus – the world is full of countries that hold "elections" under just these conditions – but not here, not yet anyway.

The second method is impersonation of eligible voters. This is a little easier, simply because it is a little less obvious but the obvious risk is that the eligible voter will have already turned up, or simply not be registered to vote. In any case, unless the polling clerk and presiding officer are very unobservant , very intimidated or very corrupt (see above for the difficulties there.) it would still be almost impossible to cast more than one vote per person, per polling station. Not impossible but still in the realms of the extremely difficult.

So was there no electoral corruption before the system changed? Yes, there was but it was necessarily limited – usually much too limited to change the course of an individual candidate's election let alone the results for a council or general election– it centred around postal and proxy voting just like most modern vote fixing and the next section will cover how it was done – before well meaning attempts to boost flagging voter turnout changed little homegrown fiddles into a major growth industry.

Election fiddling for fun and profit – The St Ives story

In 1992 the Conservative Party, under its new leader John Major won an unprecedented and largely unexpected fourth General Election victory in a row.

What is less well known is that this victory would never have happened if 1241 votes in 11 key marginals had gone the other way. In four marginals, St Ives, Bolton North East, Stirling and Tynemouth reports came in of "granny farming". (Nick Davies Guardian 09/05/2001)

Granny farming is where someone takes a proxy or postal voting form for someone else (traditionally elderly and housebound, hence the name) and then alters the intention of the voter on that form.

 For those of you who have ever been puzzled by the line "Sherriff Fatman started out in business as a granny farmer" in the eponymous Carter USM song you now know what they were talking about.

At the Pine Trees nursing home, St Ives, in 1992 17 elderly voters were persuaded to give forms applying for a postal vote to a Conservative supporter. Mysteriously, on their way to the Town Hall these all turned into applications for proxy votes to be cast by local Conservative supporters.

 Other examples, where politicians and their friends have been convicted of the same thing occurred in local elections in 1990 in Lancashire, Greater Manchester and Sheffield and in 1992 in Enfield.

All the parties knew that these things went on but they rarely actually altered any but the closest election – after all, the Conservatives were millions of votes ahead of Labour in 1992 and that *wasn't* due to electoral fraud – the Opposition parties could hardly cry "foul". (Although a fairly enjoyable thriller, "Game 10" by James Long was built around the hypothesis that the 11 key marginals had been fixed).

What kept fraud small scale was that there had to be a good reason for applying for a proxy or postal vote. Prior to New Labour, working parties had always warned against proxy or postal voting on demand for the simple reason that the opportunities for fraud were too high. Then in 1999 came the Howarth report, or to give it it's full title the Report of the Working Party on Electoral Procedures, chaired by George Howarth, Minister of State at the Home Office.

It was set up in the light of considerable concern that the turnout in the 1997 General Election had been only 71 per cent. This was the lowest since the Second World War and among the lowest in the European democracies. Fourteen years later, of course, it would be a huge improvement if we could get back to those levels of public participation. The government had in fact been elected on a manifesto which included the promise of a referendum on electoral reform. For whatever reason this referendum never happened and the Howarth report was partially a way to look for "reforms" that wouldn't actually involve changing the "first past the post" voting system but would still boost voter turnout and with it the legitimacy of those elected.

The report recommended that postal votes should be simple to obtain and available on demand. Keen to boost voter turnout the government reacted quickly by implementing the report's recommendations in the "Representation of the People Act 2000". Since then "It is no longer necessary to state a reason for applying for an absent vote, nor to obtain attestation of illness etc from a medical practitioner or an employer. Applications may be requested and allowed for an indefinite period." (Parliamentary Note snpc-03667). The specific regulations activating these provisions of the Act did not come into force until 2001.   This is when, at first almost unnoticed, Britain's vote riggers went mad.

Within a year allegations of widespread fraud had already begun. In the 2002 local elections for the Billesley ward in Birmingham Councillor John Hemmings (now a Member of Parliament) found that four invalid postal votes had been cast – in an election where the winning candidate's majority was only three – while in neighbouring Aston ward fifty postal votes were cast which had been witnessed by the same three people, not proof in itself of fraud but enough to raise eyebrows. *.)* Labour councillor Ray Race and former Lib Dem councillor Michael Hayward, both from Hampshire were both convicted of postal vote rigging in 2002. (http://news.bbc.co.uk/1/hi/england/2551157.stm) Meanwhile, in Blackburn, Councillor Mohammed Hussein (Labour) and his supporters were going around collecting blank postal voting forms from voters by deception or threat. They managed to obtain more than two hundred which they filled in with votes for Mr Hussein. Later he would receive a jail sentence of three years seven months for his actions. (Vote Rigging Crackdown, Lancashire Telegraph, 24/01/2007)

Allegations continued to fly throughout the 2003 local elections: a Conservative councillor in Guildford was jailed for forging postal ballot papers and a Liberal Democrat in Bristol was given five months for fraudulently applying for postal and proxy votes. (Joseph Rowntree Reform Trust website, *Purity of Elections in the UK. Causes for Concern.)* The Electoral Commission, while continuing to uphold the idea that postal voting had a beneficial effect on turnout now recommended to the government that (a) voters should be registered as individuals rather than by household and (b) that third parties, such as canvassers, should be prevented from handling postal ballot forms. This last was initially recommended as a law but following objections from the political parties was watered down into a guideline, with the proviso that it should become a law if it was widely ignored. (The Electoral Commission website. *The Shape of Elections to Come*) However, none of these events had much publicity or impact on public consciousness. Then came Birmingham.

BIRMINGHAM 2004

Birmingham is England's second largest city. Like London, its boundaries encompass wealthy suburbs and the deepest extremes of poverty. Ethnically and socially mixed it has played host to bitter riots during the nineteen eighties and smaller ones since. In the worst, the Handsworth riots of 1985, two men died in their blazing post office and official injury tolls came to at least 122 others, while damage to property came in at 7.5 million (The Roots of Urban Unrest Benyon & Solomos).

Historically, although high deprivation levels and the traditionally pro-Labour (until the Iraq war) loyalties of its sizeable Asian population make a handful of its inner city seats rock solid for Labour, Birmingham as a whole has usually been more politically conservative than comparable industrial metropolises. In the early 1790s the authorities in Sheffield or Norwich lived in fear that their workers, inflamed by reading "The Rights of Man", would rise and overthrow them. In Birmingham prominent Establishment figures were able to raise *anti-* democratic mobs to terrorise radicals and religious minorities under the slogan "Church and King". (Riots, Risings and Revolutions, Ian Gilmour) Perhaps it is fitting then that Birmingham was the scene of such spectacular vote rigging in the run up to the elections of June the 10th 2004 that it was the first place in Britain to be *officially* labelled worse than a "banana republic" .

The elections of 2004 were held in the context of major opposition to the Iraq war from across the population. On 15th February 2003 the biggest ever march in the whole of British history had taken place against the war. Estimates of the numbers attending ranged from a very cautious one million to a possibly over-optimistic two million plus. It was very hard to be exact because no one in Britain, not the organisers, not the authorities, not the marchers themselves had any prior experience of dealing with numbers on that scale – the closest comparison was the Notting Hill Festival, which as people are constantly coming and going and it is hard to distinguish between those deliberately attending the festival and the very substantial numbers who live in, work in or have to travel through the area is not a very close comparison at all. For a period of a few weeks following the invasion of Iraq on 20th March 2003 popular opposition in the UK had appeared to fall off but following rising troop casualties, allegations of abuse of prisoners (allegations which moved increasingly into the realms of proven fact.) and the ongoing inability to find any of the "Weapons of Mass Destruction" upon which most of the case for war had been built opposition had risen again and hardened dramatically.

Particularly worrying for the Labour government was that opposition was even higher among certain groups than in the general population. One of these groups was civil liberties campaigners. The overall numbers of these in the UK population is a matter for debate but what is not is that they are not concentrated in certain areas in large enough numbers to swing any significant number of seats.The same cannot be said of British Muslims. In inner city Birmingham, Luton, the East End of London, parts of the Black Country and the old mill towns of south Lancashire and the West Riding Muslim communities are vocal, well organised and an essential component of any Labour victory. Throw in the fact that 2004 was a mid term year anyway, traditionally bad news for the party in power and Labour was facing bitter defeat , made more galling by the fact that in some areas it was also losing support at the other end of the political spectrum to the neo-fascist British National Party.

It was in the context of this that Labour councillors and activists, many of them Muslim themselves, acted as they did. We have an advantage in considering this election that we do not have with a number of others that have been rigged in recent years in that it has been subject to an election court.

An election court does not operate quite like a normal court. It is created specifically in response to what is called an election petition, in which the petitioners formally allege that an election should be declared void. The petitioners must be either a candidate in the election just held or a group of electors (a minimum of four in local elections) from the ward where the disputed election was held. If you are neither of these then you cannot lodge an election petition, not even if the successful candidate came round to your house personally to gloat and played DVD highlights of himself stealing votes from old ladies on your flatscreen TV all night.

In the case of a local government election any petition must be lodged within 21 days of the election. It is the responsibility of the petitioners, not the Crown Prosecution Service or the police to provide the witnesses and evidence for the court. They must pay an initial fee of £400 to the elections petitions office and £50 to the Queen's Bench Master. They must have up to £2,500 in cash or assets to offer as security for costs. The petitioners will have to pay the fees for their own legal team – the bewildering array of deadlines involved alone means that it would be a very clever, well organised person or a very, very stupid one who tried to do without professional legal help and there is no guarantee at all of getting legal aid – and no time to wait and find out if you will, before lodging the petition. In addition to their own costs if the petitioners withdraw or fail to prove their case they may be ordered to pay the costs of the respondents (who will be some or all of the following: the candidate who was declared elected, the returning officer, the candidate's staff). In February 2008 an election court in Burnley ruled against the petitioners and ordered them to pay £30,000 for the respondents legal costs in a case where the number of votes had been equal and the election had been decided by drawing lots. (Lancashire Telegraph 08/02/2008). In order to win their case the petitioners must prove not only that electoral fraud has been committed *but that it affected the outcome of the election.* Simply proving that the 'winning' candidate's team deliberately broke the law with the intention of stealing the election is not enough – strong evidence must also be shown that they succeeded.

Unlike a normal court dealing with normal crime an election court can draw general conclusions as to general corruption of the electoral process in the area it investigates as well as saying "Guilty" or "Not guilty" of individuals (though it can do that as well)

Hence it is possible, under Section 164 of the Representation of the People Act 1983 to void an election for general corruption even if there is not enough hard evidence as to responsibility to pin the blame firmly to an individual or individuals. *Only* an election court can void an election. If a regular court finds a candidate guilty of a serious enough offence they may be stripped of office and a by-election held but that is not the same thing.

The bright reader will be appalled at the fact that so much is left to well meaning members of the public to do and to pay for. There are some people who would have that amount of money to hand, and the time and the organisational powers to organise a presentation to an election court in the short timescale available, and the confidence and wealth to be able to risk losing – those are the people least likely to have their votes stolen or to live in areas where it is widespread – if we ever get around to giving out medals for civic virtue then top of the list ought to be those who petitioned an election court in the Birmingham City Council elections for Bordesley Green and Aston wards in 2004 – Jamil Akhtar, Mohamed Ali, Haroon Asghar, Zulfiqat Hussain, Ayaz Iqbal, Qadeer Ahmed, Naser Iqbal.

The BNP – an interlude

Looking at those names this might be a good moment to discuss a blot on British democracy which is outside the general scope of this work but sadly must be mentioned – the British National Party. The BNP have worked tirelessly in recent years to present themselves as a democratic party. Part of this work has been a determined attempt to undermine the democratic credentials of their opponents. Electoral corruption has been a Godsend to them for several reasons. Firstly it quite genuinely *does* give grounds for concern about the commitment of some of the other parties' most active and influential members to a free and fair democratic system. Government MPs used fears of BNP Euro election victories to push through all-postal voting experiments in the 2004 European elections which were wide open to fraud. This shows a disturbing willingness to ignore potential dangers of fiddling with voting procedures so long as it frustrates the BNP. It gives that party a ready made excuse to hide its failures behind – where the BNP falters it blames fraud. In the light of what we know *has* happened it can't be proved wrong and so its propaganda is strengthened – exactly the opposite of what the government hoped to achieve. Secondly, although the BNP has had members convicted of electoral offences, the very fact of its weakness means it has far fewer examples to show than the main parties. BNP members are nowhere the political masters of council officers or police forces who should be keeping an eye out for vote rigging. The three main parties are.

   Lastly the BNP are able to point to a disproportionate number of Asians involved in ballot rigging scandals and say, in effect "Look, this is what Asians are like." In fact ballot rigging has come from people of every colour and religion and most political persuasions.   The opposition to it has as well, but disproportionately from ethnic minority activists who refuse to see their communities cheated and used as stage armies for ambitious would be "leaders".

   The politicians who opened the floodgates to election stealing and again and again failed to put effective safeguards in place are, sadly, wealthy and white almost to a man.

As for the BNP, it remains a neo-fascist party. Of its leading members, Nick Griffin has called for opposition to be dealt with by "well directed fists and boots." Nick Eriksen thinks that "Rape is simply sex" and Mark Collett thinks it would be better to live in Nazi Germany than modern day Burnley. The attacks of the BNP upon electoral fraud are a classic example of what Ignazio Silone said about the fascism of his own day "It criticises the defects and the fictions of 'bourgeois' democracy. When it comes into power it perpetuates them in an aggravated form. It criticizes the limitations imposed upon freedom of expression of opinion imposed by plutocratic forces. Under fascism liberty of expression of opinion disappears but the plutocracy remains. It criticizes the way in which party apparatuses hamper genuine self-government. Under fascism all self-government disappears. ..Fascism preserves only the apparent and superficial features of democracy – demonstrations, mass spectacles, mass..plebiscites..it presents itself in the guise of 'true democracy' being in reality only its substitute." (Ignazio Silone "The School for Dictators pp 273-274)

Returning to the question of election courts, the various court fees and expenses involved are for a single ward only. To challenge every ward in Birmingham would have cost a minimum of £18,000 in immediate fees, £100,000 to be put up as security *plus* legal fees, which at a very conservative estimate would be a minimum of £100 *per hour.*   On the basis of fees awarded in the Blackburn case (see above) it would have cost up to £1.2 million for the whole of Birmingham, not including the possibility of costs being awarded against the petitioners. Despite this, despite the fact that his specific judgements only covered the wards of Bordesley Green and Aston Mr Justice Mawrey's final report would state that "I found there was reason to believe that corrupt practices extensively prevailed in the electoral area of the relevant authority's area namely throughout the area of Birmingham City Council. "

We are lucky in the Birmingham election because politicians who have been convicted of criminal offences cannot sue those who publicise what they have done – we can speak freely about these Birmingham elections as we cannot in other cases where there is also evidence of vote rigging or general corruption. The language used by Mr Justice Mawrey in his judgements is also utterly clear and utterly unequivocal – too much so to be vulnerable to being twisted by even the best spin doctors. This, along with its sheer quotability is probably a major reason why this was by far the best publicised case of vote rigging in the last decade

The reference to the inability of a convicted politician to sue might seem a pointless truism, or even a wish for the power to spread libels until you consider that in order to convict , a criminal court must prove guilt *beyond all reasonable doubt.* Just because an individual walked free on charges of vote rigging doesn't mean they're innocent, it might simply mean that they were given the benefit of the doubt.   Now this principle is a vital protection for personal freedoms. The lawyer and novelist John Mortimer, called it the Golden Thread that runs through the British legal system, the principle that one is innocent until proven guilty and that one must be proven guilty beyond all reasonable doubt. (Rumpole and the Golden Thread). To take away this safeguard might be as bad for our freedoms as vote rigging itself. That said it should certainly be possible to devise a system that doesn't rely on individual election petitioners taking on responsibilities and expenses that ought to be the responsibility of the State itself. The civil standard of proof simply means that for a case to be decided, a judge or jury should think it is more likely than not that things happened as one side claims. The civil law is about redressing wrongs, (e.g. getting a court order to make your neighbour stop letting their noisy dog out at three in the morning) not about punishment, which is why the standard of proof is lower. If your neighbour continues to let their dog out then you can have the police on them – even though your court order is a civil matter breaking it is the criminal offence of contempt of court. As it is, it usually requires criminal standards of wrongdoing to be proved (beyond reasonable doubt still, remember) to undo or even safely report electoral wrongdoing.

The Mawrey judgement begins by going over the process of postal voting itself and pointing out the various weaknesses in the system which the fraudsters exploited.

Anyone on the electoral register can apply for a postal vote up to five working days before the election itself. In the past, with only a handful of postal voters this worked well enough. In Birmingham in 2004 seventy thousand postal votes were requested. More than forty thousand applications arrived in the thirteen days before the deadline. In the Aston ward applications for postal votes rose from five hundred and sixty to five *thousand* two hundred and forty one. In the Bordesley Green ward there were eight thousand, six hundred and forty seven applications for postal votes and more than four thousand of them arrived in the last three days. Any clever fraudster, of course, would choose to apply for postal votes close to the deadline in order to give the authorities less time to even think of investigating. The returning officer and her staff were "totally overwhelmed...This problem was particularly acute in the Bordesley Green ward" (Mawrey judgement) The irony, of course, is that the council were being overwhelmed by a flood of postal and proxy vote applications from people who had not asked for them, people who didn't live in the area, who weren't eligible to vote, who didn't want to vote, who were dead and who, in extreme cases didn't exist. Thousands of these applications were coming from eager vote riggers working all the hours God sends to steal the election. How?

"Three features of this system stand out immediately. The first is that the address to which the ballot package is sent need not be the same as the elector's address. ..Whether any thought was given to the wisdom of retaining this provision with postal voting on demand is doubtful.

The second feature is that although the application must be signed, this is, in practice, a completely useless precaution. The ERO [Electoral Registration Officer SB] does not have any specimen signature with which to compare the applicant's signature. All the ERO's staff can do is establish that there is something that appears to be a signature. Beyond that, they cannot go. The third feature is that there is no control over the way in which the application form is returned to the Elections Office....the practice has become common for canvassers of all political parties to 'sign up' postal voters and to collect the application forms for onward transmission." (Mawrey Judgement paras 39-41)

A letter is actually sent to the home address of voters when a postal vote application is received in their names – of course this is no use at all as an anti fraud measure in those cases where a fictitious name has been placed on the electoral register. Unfortunately it seems to be of very little use anyway. According to the Mawrey judgement "virtually nobody whose name is misused in this way does protest when the acknowledgement is received. The norm is to treat it as 'yet another meaningless piece of paper from the council' and to bin it." (Mawrey judgement para 42). Nor is this sort of behaviour confined to the politically apathetic – political journalist John Humphreys was prevented from voting in the 2005 General Election because he ignored just such a notice and tried to vote in person. (Guardian 3/06/2005)

Following this, the council's staff sent out the "voting packs" containing a Declaration of Identity to be signed by the voter and a witness and sealed inside an envelope together with the voter's completed ballot paper. This envelope is then placed inside *another* envelope for return to the Elections Office. This envelope was marked with purple flashes to make it easy to identify, something that was to have fateful consequences. The purpose of having a witness signature was presumably to combat fraud but this method suffers from two fatal flaws. Firstly it compromises the secrecy of the ballot. Secondly

"There are no rules as to the identity of the witness to the voter's signature. ...Provided the Declaration of Identity contains a name, something that looks like an address and something that looks like a signature of the witness, it will be treated as validly witnessed. Again, there is no mechanism for checking signatures." (Mawrey Judgement para 48)

In short there is no guarantee that the "witness" is not the "voter" using their left hand and a made up address anywhere in the world. The election staff have no way of checking and, by the time the votes arrive, no time to do so. Nor is there any rule to stop the same person witnessing hundreds of votes. In the absence of a formal complaint there is also nothing to ensure he isn't standing over the voter flanked by a brace of heavies and tapping a length of lead pipe into his palm. Unless the authorities choose to be pro-active they are unlikely to be able to stop intimidation because by definition the ones who know most about it are intimidated. *That* is *why* we had a secret ballot in the first place.

In Birmingham the vote rigging seems to have focused less on intimidation of voters than on obtaining ballot papers by hook or by crook. In those cases where postal ballot forms were being sent to addresses "controlled" by the fraudsters there was no more difficulty than that involved in filling in the forms (although as events showed there were so *many* forms that this would lead to complications later) either on their way to the voters or on their way back to the Elections Office. They were greatly aided and abbetted in this by the decision to put distinctive purple markings on the return envelopes. As Mawrey said, short of writing "Steal Me" on them nothing more could have been done to ensure that they fell into the wrong hands. Even more useful to those who stole the votes of others was the fact that if the Returning Officer receives a ballot paper on which a cross has been scribbled out and replaced with another, for another candidate *he has no powers to reject it.* Thus any completed ballot papers a thief can get hold of can be altered with impunity. A voter has cast a postal vote, a valid postal vote has arrived, and the voter has no way of knowing that their intentions were altered en route. Unless the ballot papers are brought into public scrutiny by a court, as happened in Birmingham, no one but the criminals themselves will ever know that a crime was committed.

Voting forms going to the public can be stolen by intercepting the postie or stealing mail from the hallway in the hundreds of multi-occupancy households to be found in most areas, especially inner city ones. The forms can be obtained from the voters by calling on them and taking them away – many different methods of persuasion are open here, one could claim to be a council official whose job it is to collect forms, one could offer to take them in as a party canvasser (Many members of the public do not necessarily make the distinction between party and public officials in elections) . In this context it may or may not be relevant that Ayaz Khan, one of the fraudsters ran a post office in Small Heath, putting him in an ideal position to arrange for ballots to be intercepted. Being a respected member of the community also helps – a councillor, a priest, an elder. Lastly of course, there is flat out bribery, a method which would probably work very well on the very large section of the electorate which doesn't normally vote anyway.

According to leading Liberal Democrat politician John Hemming, in previous years the going rate for a postal voting form was up to £16. Mr Hemmings was to produce photographs for the Election Court of voting packs that had been left sticking out of letter boxes to show how easy it would be for someone to go round and take them. Mr Hemmings was councillor for the neighbouring South Yardley ward where he told the court he believed at least four hundred votes had been stolen, and one of those pushing the Aston petition. He and others had alleged electoral fraud in two previous years – this together with events during the 2004 campaign including the decisions and behaviour of some of the election staff at the count itself is one of the things that triggered the decision to bring an electoral petition in the first place – many local activists and politicians in Birmingham simply seem to have felt that 2004 was the last straw.

On June 7th 2004 the first election riot in England for many years took place. The incident seems to have started on Somerville Road in the Bordesley Green area at about 7pm when a postman was seen handing over a bundle of postal ballot papers to Labour candidate Shah Jahan. At least ten people telephoned People's Justice Party candidate Shaukut Ali Khan and in a heartening display of community activism the two sides managed to muster more than two hundred supporters in the course of a few minutes. The dispute moved round the corner into Dora Road presumably on the principle of "cherchez le vote" before going toe to toe in a pitched battle which argues that whatever can be said against the voters of Birmingham apathy is not one of their faults. A witness quoted in the Birmingham Mail, who understandably wished to remain anonymous, said "Thugs and gangsters are targetting the postmen every day. Everything is getting out of control."

Elsewhere the article highlighted the case of the postman who said he had been offered five hundred pounds if he handed over his sack of ballot papers and death if he refused. Ironically, police officers were reported to be meeting with community leaders to appeal for calm, cheerfully oblivious to the fact that it was at least some of the community leaders who were the problem.

Meanwhile, in nearby Washwood Heath ward a postbox with hundreds of ballots inside was set ablaze in what was widely believed to be an attempt at destroying postal ballots that the fraudsters had failed to intercept. (Birmingham Mail June 8th 2004)

The very next evening matters took a further bizarre twist – so bizarre that some details are still hotly debated even now. In Aston ward Liberal Democrat activists Asif and Naser Iqbal were now certain that their Labour opponents were on an organised attempt to steal the election and decided to place the ward Labour HQ in Witton Road under surveillance. Sure enough, a number of key local Labour figures were seen loading cars with carrier bags and then driving off. The Iqbal brothers trailed them to the NT warehouse on the Wrylie Trading Estate. The Labour Party respondents, in their evidence, agreed with the course of events so far, but said that they had held a large number of completed ballot packages at their ward HQ due to fears about the security of the post (understandable given the burning box of Washwood Heath) but had decided to move them to a more secure place after seeing the Iqbal brothers hanging about. Shortly after all parties arrived at the warehouse the police arrived summoned by telephone, and PCs Parsons, Harrison, Bradley and Grundy and Police Sergeant   Rattenberry entered the warehouse where they found a number of Asian men sitting round a table with "hundreds" of "ballot papers with crosses on them" scattered upon it (Mawrey Judgement paras 443 – 455)

Understandably they asked for an explanation and were told that the men "were helping voters who were unable to vote because of disability or inability to speak English. They were just checking that the papers were filled in correctly." (Mawrey Judgement para 456)

Mr Justice Mawrey goes out of his way at this stage of the judgement to emphasise his belief that no blame can rightly be attached to the police officers. As they freely admitted in the witness box they knew nothing about electoral law, had never had to deal with an election in their professional capacity and had no idea of whether anything they could see might constitute a crime or not. Unspoken but very much in their minds must have been the realisation that the complainants and the men before them were all determined, well connected people capable at the very least of putting in a formal complaint. It seems
certain from their subsequent actions that this would in no way have deterred them from carrying out their duty. What seemed to be throwing them was the fact that they simply couldn't be sure, in this situation, what their duty *was*. Sergeant Rattenberry took a sample of the documents and sent two PCs off to check them. Mr Justice Mawrey believes that what the officers actually did that night was to call on a *witness* not a voter and that said witness may have been tipped off by phone.

Certainly the man the police called on was up and fully dressed at 1.30 am when PC Parsons "showed him the white piece of paper to confirm that I was at the correct address and those were his details , because I read his name off the white sheet, and then on the ballot sheet I showed him that also, to say, 'Is that your vote?' "

Mawrey says of this account "Comment seems superfluous." Apart from hoping that PC Parsons is the investigating officer if I ever commit a serious crime I can only agree. On this basis the officers decided that no crime had been committed and left. After returning to the station they raised the whole business with senior officers and were sent back to seize the documents. When they arrived several men were still there and the ballot papers now sealed in envelopes. The officers took 275 sealed envelopes back to the police station *from where they were subsequently handed to the Elections Officer, Mr Owens and counted as valid votes in the election.* (Mawrey Judgement)

The Labour respondents' explanation was that they had originally intended to place the documents in a safe at the warehouse but decided to count them first. They did not explain why, or why it took them so long, or why none of the documents ended up in the safe. Mr Justice Mawrey concluded "I have no doubt whatsoever that the three Labour Party respondents and their witnesses have told me a pack of lies." (Mawrey Report para 492) going on to say "there are only two real possibilities as to what the men present were doing:

(a)They were filling out blank ballot papers; and/or

(b)   They were examining properly completed ballot papers with a view to altering or destroying those which did not vote Labour.

Both of these practices constitute personation and consequently both constitute corrupt practices. I am quite satisfied that these men were not at the warehouse for any innocent purposes and that they were engaged in corrupt practices. "

On election day itself what might have been predicted, but wasn't, happened "Electors turned up at the polling stations in droves only to discover that their names were on the absent voters list and they were ineligible to vote." Exactly as one would expect in an election where people had suffered fradulent postal vote applications made in their name and without their knowledge. Their indignation, their ability to identify themselves, anything they said made no difference – once someone is on the absent voters list they may not lawfully vote in person unless they have a postal ballot form to hand over (which rather destroys the object of the exercise). These people had been disenfranchised twice and were only now finding out about it.

Understandably there were what Mawrey calls"ugly scenes". (Mawrey Judgement paras 269 – 271)

The Presiding Officer at Blake Lane polling station counted "at least" seventy people who were turned away. The Presiding Officer at Starbank Primary School polling station literally "lost count". These patterns were repeated at other points across the city. In some places there were also vigorous disputes between polling station staff and party observers over what the latter saw as misconduct by the election staff. Mr Justice Mawrey decided beforehand that the rights and wrongs of these disputes could not have affected the outcome of the election itself and declined, perhaps with some relief, to examine them. They are relevant to us only insofar as they helped build up a last burst of tension and ill feeling before the count itself.

The 2001 electoral regulations are very clear on how postal ballots should be handled. Once received they should be placed, unopened, into a ballot box which must then be locked and sealed. Postal votes can be counted before the election but the candidates and their agents are entitled to be present. Various procedures exist for making sure that only witnessed, signed ballots are counted and that the ballot has a unique reference number which matches that on the envelope it is sealed in. If not it would normally be marked "provisionally rejected".

In order to ensure that valid votes are not rejected due to simple confusion on the part of the staff it is the duty of the returning officer to make two lists, one of the unique numbers of ballot papers which cannot initially be matched to a declaration of identity and the second of the unique numbers of declarations of identity that cannot be initially matched to ballot papers. These can then be gone through, matching them up to validate votes wherever possible. It is usual to retain a ballot box for last minute postal votes which will be brought to the count unprocessed, locked and sealed and to bring ballot boxes full of processed ballot papers, also locked and sealed. This is not what happened in Birmingham.

As has already been said the number of postal votes in Birmingham overwhelmed the election staff. Elections Officer Mr Owens, who is fulsomely praised for his election expertise in the Mawrey judgement decided that "in order to get the maximum number of votes processed, so that no one would be disenfranchised, in order to get the election counts completed within any reasonable timescale, and lastly due to the sheer physical pressure of work on his staff that the voting regulations would be ignored.."

Consequently the two lists for matching never happened. Mr Justice Mawrey summarises the problems that arise from this as follows. " Firstly there is no 'paper trail' making subsequent audit impossible. Secondly..it vastly increases the scope for human error. ...improperly matched ballot papers can wrongly go through to the count and once in the count cannot (without an impossible amount of labour) be detected as wrongly admitted. Given the pressure under which the Elections Office team was working in the days before the poll, I consider it inevitable that this informal matching process must have led to votes being improperly admitted. How many votes it is impossible to say...." (Mawrey Judgement paras 243 – 245)

The other result of the sheer volume of postal votes and the inability of the council's staff to process them properly in the time available was that votes, processed and unprocessed, were being brought into the count in carrier bags, in bin bags, in cardboard boxes, by members of staff on foot, in the back of cars belonging to family members of election staff. It was a recipe for a collapse of public confidence. Not only were the ballot papers not secure – they were seen not to be secure.

The count itself took place at Birmingham's National Indoor Arena which had been divided into sections or "pens" for the counting of votes from each individual ward – European elections, taking place on the same day were not counted until the weekend so that results would come out at the same time as other EU states. It did not begin until the morning of the 11th June, the day after the

elections, the Birmingham authorities having decided not to try to count the votes overnight. Mawrey says "I have no doubt that this was the correct decision" (Mawrey Judgement para 276)

I on the other hand have every doubt. The first principle of elections is that they must be *seen* to be free and fair. That is why election staff seal the ballot boxes and hand them over personally to the returning officer.

That is why, until very recently the count almost always took place on election night. If votes are stored overnight they can be tampered with overnight. Someone with access to the place they were stored, a stick of sealing wax and a knack with locks could alter votes even in secured ballot boxes. In a case like this where thousands of votes were left unsecured in bags and open boxes a fraudster wouldn't even need that much – and it is surely not beyond the wit of those who are able to bribe and bully electors to think of buying and bullying council staff – especially if the fraudsters are councillors – effectively the employers of the bosses of the election staff. I am not suggesting that this did happen in Birmingham. I am saying that the possibility exists in any election where the votes are stored out of public sight. It always will. Therefore in the interests of all who believe in democracy votes should *always* be counted in plain sight and as soon as possible with no opportunity for fraudsters.

The point is given extra force by the fact that shortly after the Mawrey Judgement was handed down Elections Officer John Owens and some of his staff were suspended after *a thousand unopened postal ballots were found in the council's offices.* (Telegraph 14/04/2005) Granted this was most probably a cock-up rather than a conspiracy but it is a cock-up which would have been much less likely to happen if votes were being stored and counted properly and promptly.

Returning to the count on 11th June the sheer force of physical overcrowding must already have been fraying tempers by the time (11am) when three unlocked, unsealed ballot boxes were noticed at the Bordesley Green count. The candidates for the People's Justice Party and the Liberal Democrats became "very perturbed" at these boxes and demanded to know where they had come from, apparently in the belief that the ballot papers they contained were not lawful and should not be counted. The Senior Deputy Returning Officer took the view that they should be counted anyway. According to the Mawrey judgement he "assumed that the three boxes had arrived in the correct way". By his own evidence he made no enquiries to back up this assumption.

The Liberal Democrats brought in Councillor John Hemmings, (Since elected MP for Birmingham Yardley). The officials summoned Elections

Officer John Owens and his boss Returning Officer Lin Homer who ruled that the boxes should be opened. Again, neither of them checked the provenance of the boxes. This provoked the candidates and their agents to fury and a ferocious row ensued culminating with Ms Homer telling them "if they did not like the decision they could always bring an election petition" (Mawrey Judgement para 573) Given what happened later this looks remarkably like famous last words.

Mawrey's opinion was that the returning officer and her staff had no choice but to count the votes in the three boxes but that they should have set them aside first to check their provenance and that there was a major failure of tact and sensitivity in dealing with the candidates' concerns.

When the boxes were opened witnesses saw a remarkable number of forms filled in in the same handwriting and the same ink, invariably for Labour. The great vote rigging scam was still paying off.

At the count for neighbouring Aston ward matters had gone from bad to worse. The details of events was hotly disputed on all sides but centred around a 'Nickleby' carrier bag containing envelopes with postal ballots (everyone agrees this part), loose yellow local government ballot papers (according to the candidates but not according to Mrs Alison Harding, the Deputy Returning Officer in charge of the Aston count) and a bundle of European election ballot papers (agreed by everyone.) Mrs Harding claimed that no one objected until the votes had been processed and it was too late. Everyone else, including Mr Ahmad the council's solicitor disagrees – the votes *could* have been set aside at the time of the objections. The Election Court was unable to find a reasonable explanation for the presence of the bag or the presence of European ballot papers in it. It therefore ruled that none of the ballots from the Nickleby bag should have been counted and the decision to do so was "deplorable". In the end Mr Justice Mawrey decided he was not able to uphold complaints against the Elections Office even though the law had been broken and inadmissable votes had been counted because the petitioners had been unable to demonstrate beyond reasonable doubt that the breaches of the law by the Elections Office had affected the outcome of the elections. (Although Mawrey *did* say that the Elections Office was the author of its own misfortunes.)

This is an appalling indictment of the law as it stands, saying, in effect, that the law can freely be broken by the authorities themselves provided that private individuals with no powers of arrest, interrogation or search warrant can't prove beyond reasonable doubt that the election result was changed. *However*, despite this the elections *were* overturned because of the undoubted vote rigging the petitioners did manage to prove in the aftermath of the election.

Once the elections were over the Liberal Democrats in Aston ward and the People's Justice Party in Bordesley Green moved swiftly. They managed to scrape together the initial finance to bring an election petition – thereafter the Lib Dems were dependent upon the fact that Ayoub Khan was a legal professional who was both willing and able to do most of the work himself. The Labour Party defendants initially had the help of the party's solicitors Steel & Shamash and the PJP managed to get Legal Aid. Then, to quote Mawrey "There is no doubt that attempts were made procedurally to stifle these petitions. In particular Messrs Steel and Shamash put great pressure on the Legal Services Commission to refuse to continue funding the Bordesley Green Petitioners to trial. Although I do not suggest that they stepped over the line into legal impropriety I was very disquieted by their approach and authorised the Petitioners' solicitor to inform the Legal Services Commission that I considered it to be in the public interest that they be permitted to continue the Petition as recipients of Legal Aid." (Mawrey Judgement para 320)

We can safely assume that if Mawrey believes this to be legal it is. That said it is appalling that it should be. For solicitors for one side in a case to be able to attempt to pull the rug from under their opponents behind the scenes makes a mockery of our system of justice.

The Labour solicitors then tried to get the whole case postponed until after 5th May 2005, which at the time it was widely (and rightly as it turned out) assumed would be the date of the general election. This could be seen as an honourable attempt to avoid an election campaign being muddied with allegations whose truth or falsehood would not be confirmed until after polling day or it could be seen as a deliberate attempt on the part of the governing party to avoid embarrassment or both. Whichever it was, it failed.

Then the Labour Party respondents were thrown to the wolves by their own side. Solicitors Steel & Shamash officially informed the court that they would no longer be representing their clients. At the same time a national press release was issued saying that behaviour by some Labour activists "and supporters of other parties" may have fallen short of the high standards voters have a right to expect. This was frankly despicable on two levels.

Firstly it prejudiced the case against the Labour respondents, a case that was sub judice and secondly it attempted to gain a sly advantage, suggesting all the parties were as bad as each other, by libelling unnamed supporters of other parties, who being unnamed couldn't sue to clear the stain on the good names of their organisations.

Once the Election Court had begun a number of things became quickly clear. Firstly that large numbers of ballot papers had been altered, and by the same person. Secondly that large numbers of postal votes been received and counted purportedly from voters who it turned out had either not applied for a postal vote or had not used it. This included one man who was actually in prison at the time, removing any possibility that he may simply have forgotten about it. Thirdly that declarations of identity and signatures were falsely done in a very large number of cases by the same people signing different names and giving varying addresses. More than 1600 postal votes were cast for the Labour Party in Bordesley Green in which the signature of the voter on the application for a postal vote was not the same as the signature of the voter on the declaration of identity. (Mawrey Judgement para 386) Not one of these votes should have been accepted as valid. Every single one must be regarded as having been stolen. Evidence in the Aston ward rested largely on the "warehouse affair" and the work of handwriting experts but nevertheless the same patterns emerged, despite the ingenious defence of one Labour activist who explained that the reason he had written declarations in five different names with five different signatures giving two different addresses was because he happened to use five different versions of his name and signature and regarded two addresses as home and did fill in some names which are not his but this was purely an oversight and what was wrong with that? For the benefit of anyone who ever wants this gentleman's autograph, names used include Nazrul Islam, M H Ali, D. Ashab, Abdul Rahim, Kala Miah and B. Miah .

Mawrey found all the Labour Party respondents guilty, disqualified them from office and voided the elections for the Bordesley Green and Aston wards. He also found that the vote rigging was not the result of a handful of hotheads but was part of "a Birmingham wide campaign by the Labour Party to try, by the use of bogus postal votes, to counter the adverse effects of the Iraq war on its electoral fortunes." (Mawrey Judgement para 691) Lozells & East Handsworth, Washwood Heath, Yardley and Sparkbrook were singled out as other likely fraud hotspots.

Mawrey lamented that "This court..cannot set aside the election in any other ward of Birmingham City Council; [because petitions were only brought for Bordesley Green and Aston wards – SB] still less can it require the entire election to be re-run." (Mawrey Judgement para 679)

Having noted that none of the police officers who appeared before him were to be blamed for the failure of the police force to tackle electoral fraud Mawrey went out of his way to emphasise both the unwillingness and the inability of the police to deal with vote rigging "there is a marked reluctance on the part of the police to involve themselves in electoral matters....This not helped by the invidious position in which a police force is put when investigating electoral fraud in a local authority context. The alleged fraudsters may, after all, be members of the political authority to which the force is answerable...In the case of the Birmingham elections of 2004 the attitude of the West Midlands police to allegations of fraud could, at the kindest, be described as one of Olympian detachment...In the course of the election the police were presented with a large number of complaints. Mr Hemming himself told me he had presented some fifty dossiers to the police. The reaction of the police can be best summed up by drawing attention to the codename they gave to the complaints of malpractice – *Operation Gripe.* This indicates better than anything else their view that the whole business was a waste of their time and that Mr Hemming and the other complainants were a tiresome nuisance. " (MawreyJudgement paras 147 – 150)

Mawrey concluded of the police that "If an open and shut case is presented to them, they will act and act promptly but they cannot and, it seems, will not be remotely proactive." (Mawrey Judgement para 157). Others, considering what happened at the warehouse where police officers were presented with ongoing fraud in front of their eyes and failed to act may wonder just how much more open and shut a case could get and conclude that nothing short of storming a polling station and burning the ballot boxes could have moved the police to effective action.

More damning than anything anyone could have said is the fact that the West Midlands police force failed miserably to take any effective action even though ordinary members of the public knocking on doors and hiring a handwriting expert proved able to build a case "beyond reasonable doubt". Nothing could have shown them up more.

Mawrey concluded that the *only* real safeguard against electoral fraud was the Election Petition and that even this was no real safeguard in any except the rarest of cases because of the expense and difficulties involved.

It was shortly before Mawrey's final judgement was handed down that a government statement was issued saying "The systems already in place to deal with allegations of electoral fraud are clearly working." Mawrey's response deserves quoting in full.

"Anybody who has sat through the case I have just tried and listened to evidence of electoral fraud that would disgrace a banana republic would find this statement surprising. To assert that 'The systems already in place to deal with allegations of electoral fraud are clearly working' indicates a state not simply of complacency but of denial.

"The systems to deal with fraud are not working well. They are not working badly. The fact is that there are *no* systems to deal realistically with fraud and there never have been. Until there are, fraud will continue unabated." (Mawrey Judgement paras 715 – 717)

(Mawrey may or may not have been aware that a commission in the nineteen forties had also come to the conclusion that there were no adequate mechanisms to combat electoral fraud and had recommended the creation of a public post with wide ranging powers to replace the Election Petition system. Sadly this recommendation was never implemented.)

One sequel to the case should be mentioned here. One of the Labour respondents, Mr Afzal, managed to persuade the High Court that he had not *personally* committed or had knowledge of wrongdoing and was thus able to stand again for Labour in the 2007 council elections as a man who couldn't spot massive organised fraud on the part of his closest political allies going on under his nose but was nevertheless not a crook. Following a bitter campaign in which it was alleged that his opponent was guilty of falsely claiming benefits and electoral fraud Mr Afzal was elected once more to Birmingham City Council. Clearly you can't keep a good man down.

The judgement was widely reported, coming as it did in the middle of a general election campaign especially as only a few days later a former Labour councillor in Blackburn was jailed for stealing votes in much the same manner as in Birmingham. Luckily the government had an immediate plan. It was to deny that there was an issue.

Peter Hain, then Leader of the House of Commons told GMTV "..you're talking about tiny isolated examples of fraud here...There were, I think 1500 votes involved in the fraud case in Birmingham recently compared to 7.7 million [nationally].. So there's fraud that has to be tackled and we have to look all the time at improving the system and we'll take advice from the Electoral Commission." (Guardian 11 April 2005)

There are quite a few things that could be said to this. The first is that the government had already had advice from the Electoral Commission that postal voting, especially as currently constituted was open to fraud and it had ignored it. The second is that the Electoral Commission had wanted it to become standard practice for all postal vote applications to go via the returning officers. The parties had refused to agree so this had been watered down to a "guideline". At the very moment the Mawrey Judgement was handed down all three main party leaders were sending letters to voters across the country urging them to return postal vote applications to addresses controlled by the parties themselves. Mr Blair's 'personal' letter to voters gives an address for a 'Postal Votes Centre' which Guardian reporters found to be Labour's communication headquarters (Guardian 15/04/2005)

Another point of course, is that the Minister is using what can only be deliberately misleading figures. The 1500 votes he refers to were in *one* ward, one of only two that were properly investigated – if they were projected across the nation (just a bit of fun) the equivalent figure would be more than two million two hundred thousand ballots. The only way to be certain would be to investigate properly and that is exactly what the government chose not to do. Despite Mawrey's cry from the heart they did not investigate any other Birmingham wards.

More than anything Labour ministers could say, the party's real attitude is shown by the fact that none of the Labour activists and councillors involved were expelled from the Labour Party. The same government that had created the loopholes making widespread electoral fraud possible was denying there was a problem whilst wearing its government hat and refusing to take action whilst wearing its party hat. It certainly wouldn't have been difficult to do. Once the election was done Labour had an election free gap of nearly a year to work in. Labour's leaders had built up enormous powers to expel members over the course of the nineteen-eighties and nineties.

Among those expelled had been Militant members who fervently believed that Labour MPs, representing working people, should live on the average wage of a skilled worker . A few score expulsions later such views are anathema amongst Labour MPs who mostly seem to think they don't get paid enough.

The message sent to vote riggers by the courts is increasingly that vote rigging is a serious crime. The message sent to vote riggers by parties that don't expel members for it is "Don't get caught"

What is more, there was no investigation at all into the results of the European elections. The stolen voting packages in Birmingham and elsewhere had contained ballot papers for the European elections as well as the local ones. We know that some of these turned up at the local election count in Birmingham where they should never have been.

It was no part of Mawrey's brief to look at European ballots but is it really conceivable that the men who stole thousands of local votes would not have used the Euro ballot papers that came with them for political advantage? Just to ask the question shows the absurdity of the idea. Whether there were enough votes stolen to change the European election results is an open question – the electoral system used for EU elections is more proportional and thus harder to affect with a few strategically placed ballots - but that fraudulently obtained votes were cast seems as certain as anything in this fallen world can be.

Despite all this it would not be until 2006 that any changes to the system were made at all – and subsequent court cases would prove how ineffective these new safeguards were, but before coming to those we must take a look at the 2004 European elections before we move into the sound and fury of the 2005 General Election where yet again the spectres of fraud and general skulduggery would raise their increasingly familiar heads.

European Elections 2004

The European elections of 2004 were notable for the fact that in four regions, the North West, Yorkshire and Humberside, East Midlands and the North East postal voting was no longer available on demand – it was compulsory.

The government's idea was to scotch "extremists", specifically the British National Party by increasing the turnout. It seems to have given little thought to the fact that three years before the proudly 'extreme' Sinn Fein had won three parliamentary seats on the highest turnout in the country (Telegraph 22/03/04). The Electoral Commission was in favour of a pilot in two regions but balked at four – covering nearly fifteen million electors the pilot had gone beyond being a pilot and appeared to be on the verge of overloading the plane. The House of Lords agreed with the Electoral Commission but the government decided to press ahead anyway.

When the turn out rose, hitting 38 per cent in the all-postal areas the government claimed it had been vindicated. Many were not so sure. As we have seen in Birmingham an apparent rise in turnout is actually one of the signs of vote stealing as fraudsters vote in the names of people who wouldn't otherwise have bothered or would have been unable to do so, being abroad, in prison, non existent or dead.

In the areas where voting in person was still possible what the Electoral Commission describes as a "small" number of voters arrived to vote but were refused because they were on the list of voters who had applied for a postal vote. "Some were intending voters who had agreed to tick a box requesting a postal vote as a result of political parties' campaigning activities, without realising the significance of their actions.

One elderly lady told an Electoral Commission observer 'I just agreed to do it (tick the box) to get the party canvasser to go away. I didn't realise it meant I wouldn't be able to vote at the polling station.' " (Electoral Commission Official Report on the 2004 European Parliamentary elections in the UK) It would be very instructive to know how small this number was. As the Electoral Commission certainly didn't have observers at all polling booths and as it seems unlikely it would have been mentioned in an otherwise frankly anodyne report if it was an isolated incident, the 'small' number of these cases may have been enough to swing a number of seats. Even if it wasn't ,British citizens were still being disenfranchised through no fault of their own – a fate previously reserved for royalty and the certifiably insane. The number of voters turned away because a postal vote had been applied for in their names and without their knowledge certainly wasn't small in certain wards in Birmingham, as we know. It would be even more instructive to know if the elderly lady's postal ballot was cast, and who for, and in whose handwriting. In the absence of an official enquiry we are unlikely ever to find out.

Of course, incidents of this kind were only possible in the nine regions where voters could go to a polling station and find out that their votes had been taken. In the all-postal regions of the Midlands and the North what had happened in Birmingham's local elections could happen with far fewer warning signs. No one would be turned away from polling stations, no one was able to prove that someone else had applied for a postal vote on their behalf, and given ongoing problems with the printing and posting of ballots which the Electoral Commission's report highlights no one could prove that their voting forms had gone astray due to theft, as opposed to simple bad luck.

Under these circumstances the chances of anyone taking the financial risk of bringing an Election Petition were always going to be minimal – unless they were lucky enough to stumble across another voting factory like the one in Birmingham they would have nothing but guesses to base it on. The same would apply to complaining to the police. Barring a public enquiry, all-postal voting was a surefire scrutiny proof zone for fraudsters. Far from offering what minister Nick Raynsford called "a useful, practical alternative to traditional polling stations." (Press Release

21/01/2004) it was a classic example of what the Select Committee on Home Affairs was warning against when it said "Change must not be allowed to threaten the integrity of the election process..Change must not be introduced to a system which works well simply for change's sake." (Select Committee on Home Affairs 1998: Fourth Report: Electoral Law and Administration.) Or to put it more colloquially "If it ain't broke don't damn well go fixing it!"

The Electoral Commission report 'Delivering Democracy' on the future of all postal ballots is a broadly optimistic document with a touching faith that postal ballots increase democratic participation. It follows the 2003 report 'Absent Voting in Great Britain' in which, it will be remembered, the Commission recommended pilots with a view to making all postal ballots the standard method for local elections. By 2004 the Commission had done a U turn. And despite the report's overall optimism it does include a section on the integrity of the process. Most allegations "relate either to voters being coerced to vote a certain way, or to voters being coerced into handing over their uncompleted ballot paper for completion by someone else. There is also concern over the integrity of the electoral register." (Delivering Democracy para 4.83) The report goes on to say that "we are aware of only two investigations that have resulted in arrests to date. In Oldham three men have been arrested in connection with stealing ballot papers and in Halton [in Cheshire SB] there have been two arrests for forgery. There have also been well publicised allegations in other parts of the pilot regions such as Burnley, Sheffield, Derby and Bradford but it is too soon to know if any of these will result in prosecution." (Delivering Democracy para 4.84)

To spare readers the suspense there were successful convictions for vote rigging of Liberal Democrat councillors in Burnley, and of Conservative activists in West Yorkshire. The Derbyshire police forwarded a file to the CPS recommending prosecution, with no apparent result and in Halton several people including Labour councillor and former Mayor Patrick Tyrell were convicted of breaching the law although the judge accepted, at least in Mr Tyrell's case that the offences were technical, rather than a deliberate attempt to steal votes. Nothing more was ever heard of Sheffield so presumably either Sheffield's electoral doings are clean enough to eat your dinner off (a welcome change from 1990 when a Liberal Democrat was convicted of forging votes.) or Sheffield's criminals are too clever to leave evidence trails.

Certainly a great many people who were in a good position to know thought that electoral fraud *had* gone on, including the Labour MPs Marsha Singh and Ann Cryer both of whom were convinced that pressure was being put on young people and women, especially in "traditional"Asian households to put their votes in the hands of the head of the household.

Again, as we asked in the last chapter, why would those stealing votes for their party in the local elections *not* steal votes in the European elections when they had the ballot papers in their hands?

It seems almost certain that votes were stolen in the European elections of 2004 and, to quote Mawrey again, "If there are virtually no means whereby fraud can be brought to light and sanctioned, then 'hard evidence' of fraud is inevitably going to be scarce. Whether in those circumstances it is prudent (or even honest) to regard absence of hard evidence as proving that the problem does not exist is, of course, another question entirely." (Mawrey Judgement para 166). The all postal ballots effectively made any specifically Euro election related fraud "invisible". It may be some years before we will be able to get a clear look at Euro fraud in the era of postal voting on demand.

Incidents in the General Election of 2005

The General election of 2005 was always going to be a rough ride for the government. In addition to the usual risks involved in having been the incumbent long enough to give the electorate a chance to get bored this was the first General Election to be held since the invasion of Iraq.

After two years of war and occupation, casualties amongst British troops and the Iraqi people both were mounting alarmingly. It was now obvious to everyone except the Prime Minister, Tony Blair, and a dwindling number of his closest loyalists that Weapons of Mass Destruction were never going to be found.

To give them credit the government had fought back against its critics.

The innocent Dr David Kelly had been exposed as a journalistic source and then literally hounded to death. The journalist Andrew Gilligan had been publically crucified over a tiny inaccuracy in an overwhelmingly accurate report , by a cabal of from the highest reaches of government, including those paragons of honest virtue Alistair Campbell and Tony Blair, who had aided and abetted the deaths of uncounted thousands. The government, on the basis of a tiny and arguable inaccuracy, broadcast once, had used the conclusions of a non-statutory enquiry headed by the handpicked judge Lord Hutton, to force the resignation of the Director General of the BBC Greg Dyke. By any standards this was an unprecedented triumph for any post war government in the unending Ourobos battle between government and media, especially since most of the public, as far as can be judged, were *against* the government.

Luckily for the government the opposition Conservative party, a few dissidents notwithstanding, had also backed the war and was in no position to make capital out of its growing unpopularity.

The Liberal Democrats had opposed the invasion of Iraq but had then backpedalled somewhat after the war had actually begun for fear of being seen as unpatriotic – nevertheless they could reasonably hope to pick up votes and seats. However, due to the vagaries of the UK's electoral system they and everyone else knew that they would almost certainly be unable to win or even come second – in the end their 23 per cent of the votes cast would win them fewer than ten percent of the seats in Parliament.

That left various dissident groups and individuals which offered no threat at all of overturning the government but had every chance of costing individuals their seats and causing huge embarrassment.

One of these was Reg Keys whose son had been murdered in an ambush in Iraq and he had targetted the Prime Minister's own seat in Sedgefield, aided and abetted by Bob Clay, the fiercely left wing former Labour MP. In the end he would win 4,252 votes – over ten percent – and his bitterly eloquent speech from the platform on election night highlighting how the soldiers of his son's unit had died because of faulty and inadequate equipment cannot have made pleasant hearing for the PM no matter how relieved his victory had made him.

Rose Gentle was another parent whose son had been killed in action, and like Reg Keys she blamed the government. Although she only won 1,513 votes her campaign against Armed Forces Minister Adam Ingram was a well publicised running thorn in the government's side.

In Blackburn the Home Secretary Jack Straw faced former British Ambassador to Uzbekistan, Craig Murray, running as an independent. Craig Murray, a firm believer that the invasion of Iraq was illegal, had been edged out of his post after strongly criticising Britain's friendship with the Uzbek regime. Unlike the leader of the neighbouring regime in Turkmenistan the Uzbek dictator had at least stayed sane enough not to have named a month of the year after his mother. Equally unhinged and much less funny however was the Uzbek government's habit of boiling suspected opponents alive. Craig Murray had argued strongly that this was not a regime to be friendly with and had also accused MI6 of getting information from torture carried out by the Uzbek government.

Elsewhere, primarily Birmingham Sparkbrook and the East End of London the government was being challenged by the anti-war party Respect. Respect had been founded with the object of giving political expression to the anti war movement and represented a broad coalition of Muslim and far left groups, notably the Socialist Workers Party. Its best known member was the MP George Galloway who had been expelled from the Labour Party for his opposition to the invasion of Iraq.

Unfortunately for him he was famous for having toasted Saddam Hussein with the words "Sir, I salute your courage, your strength and your indefatigibility.".

Unfortunately for Labour MP Oona King who he was running against in Bethnal Green and Bow he didn't appearto care and if the 2004 local election results were anything to go by, neither did large numbers of her constituents.

Indeed the reason for Respect selecting Bethnal Greenand Bow to run in, unlike campaigns in Sedgefield or Blackburn seemed to be simply the very large level of anti war feeling there, rather than the particular crimes of the local MP who, albeit a war supporter , had done no more than hundreds of others. The campaign was to be a bitter one. Both Galloway and sitting MP Oona King were to be subjected to death threats in the course of it. Ms King was in a particularly difficult position as she had not initially been freely selected by her local party at all but had been one of a list of "approved" candidates vetted by Labour's leadership. (Oona King, House Music)

In the midst of the General Election, on 4th April 2005 came the results of the Election Court at Aston and Bordesley Green. The press had been reporting allegations from the trial for months (eg Times 23rd February 05) – now came proof that they were true. In March the Parliamentary Select Committee on Constitutional Affairs had called for voters to be registered individually, rather than by household as a protection against possible electoral fraud – the government had not reacted, arguing that it was too close to the General Election to start changing the way the system worked. As we have seen, the Electoral Commission had urged the action a year before and been declined. A flurry of articles hit the press highlighting the potential risks of electoral fraud and ministers hit the studios to argue that there wasn't an issue – a difficult task given that 15 per cent of all votes cast in the election would turn out to be postal votes - more than enough to swing the election. Clearly if these turned out to be vulnerable there was a very, very big problem. The government said that extra resources had been given to police to tackle voting fraud. Chris Fox of the Association of Chief Police Officers told the Independent on Sunday (IoS 10/04/2005) no police force had actually received anything extra.

A couple of days after the Birmingham verdicts a former Labour councillor from Blackburn was jailed for vote rigging in a 2002 election using much the same methods as others had used in Birmingham (BBC News 08/04/2005)

Craig Murray told the Times that he would write to the Electoral Commission because he believed the election in Blackburn simply wasn't safe

" I've been approached by several people in the Asian community who are under huge pressure from Labour activists to apply for a postal vote rather than a ballot vote and then hand over their postal vote to the Labour Party. This is happening now in Blackburn on a wide scale. In my career as a diplomat I've been used to precisely this situation abroad but wasn't expecting to face it in the UK." (Times 10/04/2005)

Lest anyone think Mr Murray was motivated simply by pique at having been forced out of his job it should be noted that the Conservative and Lib Dem candidates made similar allegations. (Telegraph 06/05/2005)

Even a Labour MP, Marsha Singh who sits for the Yorkshire seat of Bradford West was moved to say "I warned that postal voting would lead to cash and carry democracy. The government says it will increase voter turnout but with it we are sacrificing the sacrosanct principle of democracy, which is the secret ballot." (Times 10/04/2005)

As it turned out Mr Singh had every reason to fear electoral fraud. Within a few days Marsha Singh's Conservative opponent and several of his associates were to be arrested for vote rigging. Since then although the candidate himself has been discharged five Conservative activists, two of them former councillors have been convicted of what the judge described as "an organised attempt to rig the voting system" and jailed in a series of trials that lasted until 2010. (Bradford Telegraph and Argus 'Bradford Councillors Were Among Group That Conspired To Change Ballot Outcome' 07/09/2010)

Nor was Mr Singh alone – Ann Cryer, the Labour MP for Keighley expressed the hope that the Birmingham verdicts "might deter certain persons in my constituency who were scurrying round harvesting ballot papers last May. Those people were from all three major parties...I received numerous complaints from my constituents last year, and the same sort of thing also happened in two of the Bradford constituencies." (Hansard 05/12/2005 Column 1287)

Despite this, as we have seen the three main parties and a number of Labour affiliated unions went ahead and ignored the recommendations of the Electoral Commission, harvesting votes by persuading voters to send them to party "controlled" addresses, or simply to hand them over on the doorsteps. Opposition leader Michael Howard attacked the government for undermining the integrity of the electoral system but events in Bradford and elsewhere were soon to show that vote rigging wasn't confined to any one party.

The Evening Standard newspaper got one of its reporters to obtain ten postal votes by deception simply in order to show how easy it was to do. In a fit of genius the Metropolitan Police decided the appropriate response was to investigate the Evening Standard.

Those of you who might think this decision unprecedented would be quite wrong – in the nineteenth century a radical journalist working with the Salvation Army bought a teenage girl for immoral purposes solely to prove that there needed to be stronger laws against such things. Far from harming her he placed her with a family of Salvationists and published the story to the world, forcing a drastic change in the law and was surprised to be prosecuted by the very authorities he had alerted. (The Case of Eliza Armstrong, Alison Plowden 1974). It was widely suspected at the time that this was simply revenge on the part of those in highplaces – one of the brothels which were exposed was reputed to be patronised by members of more than one Royal family. No such motive can possibly exist in this case of course. Nevertheless the Met took until June to announce that they were dropping the case and then the reason they gave was that "there was insufficient evidence to prosecute." (Guardian 03/06/2005)

We can only hope that they were lying in order to back gracefully out of the ridiculous situation they had put themselves into. If the police are really unable to find evidence that has been printed in a national newspaper it's time to go back to the days of the Bow Street Runners.

On a more serious note it casts serious doubt on the decision at about the same time by the West Midlands police to abandon further investigation into alleged electoral frauds in Birmingham and Wolverhampton.

Back to April 05 and Birmingham Liberal Democrat John Hemming who had been a driving force behind the decision to bring the election petitions in Bordesley Green and Aston was making a determined attempt to halt the whole general election unless postal voting on demand could be stopped. Mr Hemming was again trying to use a clause in the European Convention on Human Rights guaranteeing free and fair elections by secret ballot.

Article 3 of Protocol 1 states "The High Contracting Parties [that is, the governments of the EU SB] undertake to hold free elections at reasonable intervals by secret ballot , under conditions which will ensure free expression of the opinion of the people in the choice of the legislature." and Mr Hemmings was attempting to argue that the election was neither free nor fair and effectively no longer secret on the basis of the massive shortcomings which had been exposed by the Mawrey Judgement. His case was turned down on the grounds that it was impossible to say in advance that an election would not be free and fair and therefore he must come back after the General Election with any evidence then. An earlier attempt by Mr Hemming to achieve the same end had been turned down on similar grounds in 2002, together with the comment that "judicial review, as sought is not even arguably, an available remedy" (www.stolenvotes.org.uk) - clearly the Mawrey judgement was being taken as a "one off" rather than evidence of the need for change, or perhaps the court was simply stating its belief that it did not have the power to look at election law. If it doesn't it is hard to see who does other than the politicians who wrote the law in the first place.

What would be interesting to know is if either the learned judge or Mr Hemmings himself were aware of the report from the European Commision for Democracy Through Law (Venice Commision) published on 18/03/2004.

This report looks specifically at remote voting, whether by post, by proxy or by some form of e voting and sets out a code of best practice. It concludes that Article 3 does not of itself either automatically ban or automatically permit remote voting but does impose minimum standards for meeting the security and secrecy of the ballot. One example it gives of a safeguard is a voter's declaration that they have filled out their postal vote themselves and in secret as required in Germany, but does not stop to consider the worthlessness of this if a voter has been bribed or intimidated, nor any means of making sure that the person filling out the declaration *is* a legitimate voter. The report *does* however state that "postal voting should only be allowed if the postal system is safe and reliable." (Venice Commission para 65) and that "Fraud and intimidation must not be possible"(para 15). For this reason, together with the danger of what the report calls "family voting" the report recommends "These practices [postal and proxy voting SB] should not be encouraged inthe new democracies.."

One can only wonder what they would have said if they had known that within a few weeks of their report, postal workers would be being bribed and threatened in Birmingham, letter boxes being burned and riots taking place to gain control of postal voting forms. Under the circumstances it is very hard to see them certifying theUK postal system as either "safe" or "secure"

Times journalist Dominic Kennedy who had provided much of the work for the Times' campaign to highlight the issues over postal ballots was quoted as saying

"There is obviously a terrible problem with intimidation. When I went to Yorkshire and the North West last June, I found people in vulnerable communities routinely forced to show their postal vote to bullies to prove who they voted for. This could be a frail girl who is physically intimidated, or a Pakistani man who speaks no English and has been ordered by his boss to vote Labour or be sacked." (Times 26/03/2005)

Times columnist and former MP Matthew Parris says on this topic "Ask the police why they are doing nothing and they will say they have spoken to people who they describe as "community leaders" who say there is no problem. Well there's a surprise." (Times ibid)

To be fair to the police one of the major problems with intimidation is that its victims are too afraid to come forward. Another factor inhibiting those from an Asian background, according to Liberal Democrat politician Parmit Singh Gill, who alleged undue pressure was being used on voters in his constituency by so-called community leaders, was fear of damaging the community's good name.

Nor was fraud confined to the inner cities or the urban north. On 22/03/05 the Thames Valley police confirmed that there had definitely been electoral fraud in the Redlands ward in Reading in the previous year's local elections but that they had no way of tracing the perpetrators. By this time of course it was months too late for an electoral petition so the 'losing' candidates could do nothing more than call for their Labour opponent to step down and hold a by-election. He, of course declined, while Reading Borough Council's Chief Executive, Trisha Haines said that "we are now sure that the postal voting irregularities did not have an impact on the overall results of the election" – even though the council was unable to state the exact number of fraudulent votes cast nor for which party. Conservative and Liberal Democrat politicians did not agree. Chief Superintendent Murray was quoted as saying

"It would have been lovely to have caught somebody but anybody who might contemplate voting malpractices in future there is a clear message that the audit from the local authority will pick it up and we will investigate it." (Reading Evening Post 23/03/2005.)

Well, yes. There is also a clear message that the election results will be allowed to stand even though fradulent voting has been exposed, and that the perpetrators have got clean away with it. Any rational ballot rigger considering the message of Reading will probably conclude that it is definitely worth carrying on.

In the meantime the flamboyant George Galloway and his supporters had discovered what they believed to be evidence of organised vote rigging in Tower Hamlets. In large numbers of properties voters were registered who didn't live there. In some of these cases no one lived at the property and yet up to a dozen postal votes in varying names had been issued to the address. What the Evening Standard called "a fairly cursory examination" threw up "a dozen" suspicious cases "six Bangladeshis apparently living in the same flat as two Irish people, eight more living in a two room bedsit. At Pat Shaw house, an old peoples home in Globe Road, most of the residents seem to have at least two votes each, often under subtle variations of their names: for instance Elsie Fernie and Elsie Ferniel, Derek Hall and Dereck Hall, Joseph Swerner and Joseph Swerwer. There is no suggestion that these people are fraudsters but are these old people being exploited by vote stealers? Or could it simply be exceptionally incompetent clerical work that no one has bothered to check?" (Evening Standard Exposed: Brick Lane's vote riggers)

The journalist wisely leaves the question hanging: sometimes silence is eloquent.

The article goes on to report further allegations "A Bangladeshi couple called the Begums told me, through an interpreter how they had been twice visited by an activist from one of the main political parties – not Respect or Labour. This man, also a Bangladeshi , demanded that the Begums hand over their completed postal votes, saying that it was their duty to him as an elder of the community...Luckily the Begums have a teenage daughter born and brought up in Britain, English-speaking and so not schooled in deference to authority. 'I argued with him,' she said 'I told him to get lost. It was obvious he was just going to take my parents' votes'. The activist harangued Mr and Mrs Begum saying their daughter was being disrespectful and they were humiliating themselves as parents by taking orders from her. But he eventually withdrew...Who knows how many other Bangladeshi families – not blessed with spirited teenagers – have lost their votes in this way?

"And then there is the vexed question of council funding. On the record Rana Miah, a member of the management committee of theBrick Lane Youth Development Association (Blyda) tells the Standard that two Labour councillors have threatened his colleagues that if they do not vote for King in the election their funding is at risk." (Evening Standard)

Oona King condemned the threats as "scandalous" but admitted "It's been a problem in the past." (Evening Standard) Nevertheless Bethnal

Green remained one of the many constituencies where Labour collected postal votes.

A spokesperson for Oona King said, quite correctly, that this wasn't illegal, (Socialist Review May 05) but in an area where the MP *admits* that councillors put unlawful pressure on voters it is reckless to say the least.

The constituency of Bethnal Green and Bow got more than its fair share of attention for a number of reasons, not least the fact that it was within easy reach of work and home for journalists on the major papers but there is no reason to suppose that what went on there did not also happen in other threatened Labour seats.

Meanwhile, far to the north, independent candidate Craig Murray had discovered that his New Labour opponent Jack Straw was literally holding a banquet for his Muslim supporters – free food provided. This, of course, is the offence of "treating" at least if a court decided that the intention had been to influence anyone's vote – and what other motive is there likely to be for holding a banquet in the middle of an election campaign? Once very common, treating was outlawed by the Great Reform Act of 1832 and gradually stamped out over the years until it had become unheard of. (Who says New Labour has no sense of history?) If convicted Jack Straw would have automatically forfeited election and been banned from public office as well as risking a prison sentence of up to two years. It is what is known as an offence of strict liability, that is to say, the candidate is liable even if his supporters were to organise the banquet without his knowledge. In this case however the issue didn't arise – Jack Straw was the keynote speaker. Not wishing to look a gift horse in the mouth Murray took his evidence to the police who in turn sent a dossier to the Crown Prosecution Service.

The sequel is fascinating. The CPS sent back to Lancashire police saying they would not be prosecuting, but rather than give the usual reasons, that there was insufficient evidence to realistically justify prosecution they said that the offence was "trivial". There is no such thing as an offence so 'trivial' that it ceases to be a crime.

It is possible that a CPS lawyer or caseworker inexperienced in electoral law (as most lawyers are, since for so many years electoral offences were vanishingly rare) misunderstood the provisions of the law and thought that, as with an election petition there would need to be evidence not only that an offence had been committed but that it had swayed the outcome of the election. This would be a mistaken interpretation of the law but an understandable mistake and Blackburn is a safe enough Labour seat that it would take a lot more than one banquet to swing it. Unfortunately this is not necessarily the case.

The Crown Prosecution Service was brought into being by the Prosecution of Offences Act 1985 and has been losing friends ever since. Its function was to take decisions on prosecution out of the hands of the police and into the hands of a supposedly more neutral body.

The Code upon which the CPS operates states that for a case to be prosecuted "there must be a realistic prospect of conviction". This is a much higher threshold than the old rule which was that there should be a prima facie (on the face of it – SB) case to answer. Inevitably this code leads to CPS caseworkers, usually junior grade civil servants, many with little or no legal knowledge or training, burdened with heavy caseloads and targets who have only a written file to go on making decisions which would previously have been made by judges, juries and magistrates. The various evidential criteria listed for the caseworker to use are subjective enough that the widely respected crime journalist David Rose has summed them up as "having read the case file the prosecutor should act on a hunch." (In the Name of the Law, David Rose,1996)

Worse, there is a second criterion which can be used to retreat from prosecution. The caseworker must decide if continuing to pursue a case is "in the public interest". In 1994 more than 28 per cent of all discontinued cases were dropped "in the public interest".

The definition of public interest used by the Crown Prosecution Service is that given by former Attorney General Lord Hartley Shawcross. A man whose integrity and loyalty were rarely questioned, Hartley Shawcross defended mine owners whose workers had been killed in an industrial disaster (266 men perished in one day – the enquiry found a series of management failures), was elected to Parliament as a Labour

MP, sat as a crossbench peer in the House of Lords and eventually joined the SDP.

Shawcross, as Attorney General, in 1951 had ruled that prosecution of crime was not automatic but account must be taken of "the effect which the prosecution, successful or unsuccessful as the case may be, would have upon public morale and order, and with any other considerations affecting public policy"(Rose, op.cit)

This is the criterion of public interest used by the CPS. Itis clearly not just a legal opinion but a political one. It offers a massive get out for CPS workers who can see that they are in a difficult situation.

It also elevates "public morale...order..public policy" above more mundane things such as guilt, innocence and truth which the more naive of us thought were what the court process was supposed to be about.

Put yourself in the position of whatever poor clerk received the dossier from Lancashire police. The evidence is not in doubt and nor is the law. Probably a good lawyer could find a defence for the Home Secretary, possibly there is evidence yet to be uncovered which would prove him completely innocent, but to assume that is not a CPS caseworker's duty or right. The trouble is that the CPS was, at that time, part of the Home Office. Jack Straw, Home Secretary, was not the boss of whoever considered the case against him – he was their boss's boss's boss and then some. Someone in that position doesn't have to use his power to influence someone's career – eager minions all the way down the line will do it for them, with or without his knowledge or prompting.

Only someone of almost suicidal integrity would have recommended prosecution, knowing that their manager, or their manager's manager or the Home Secretary's private office, or the Attorney General, or *someone* was likely to step in and rule that the prosecution wasn't in the public interest leaving Straw scot-free and a black mark on their record.

It may be that someone of great integrity did take the decision, totally uninfluenced either conciously or unconciously by the fact of the accused being the second or third most powerful man in England and their own ultimate employer, using the same criteria they would bring to bear upon any case and decided that the illegal "treating" of voters during an election really wasn't important, or that a prosecution would undermine public order and morale, or public policy. Somehow that prospect is even worse.

Meanwhile the election carried on, eventually returning Blair's New Labour to government with an overall majority of 66 seats. This was despite the fact that Labour won only 35.3 per cent of all votes cast – only 21.6 per cent of the total electorate. It was the lowest vote for any government in British history that held a majority of Commons seats. In England itself the Conservatives polled approximately seventy thousand votes *more* than Labour but won ninety two seats *fewer* . Clearly vote rigging is not the only thing wrong with the UK's electoral system.

On election night itself the police were called in after forty-three postal ballots with no declarations of identity mysteriously made their way into the Stoke North count.

In Bethnal and Bow Respect turned a majority of more than ten thousand for Labour's Oona King into an eight hundred and twenty three vote majority for George Galloway. In a bitterly triumphant acceptance speech Galloway again accused his opponents of fraud and lashed out at the Returning Officer, demanding her resignation. (House Music – the Oona King Diaries, 2007) Obviously, however, there was no likelihood now of Respect being the ones who would bring an election petition which would reveal the existence or extent of any vote rigging in the constituency. Even, or perhaps especially, if you think your opponent cheated, no politician will spend money and effort challenging an election they won.

There *was* an attempt to bring an election petition in Bethnal Green and Bow – around fifteen hundred residents of Bow had been left off the electoral register – a larger number than Galloway's majority, in the unlikely event that they would all have chosen to vote and vote the same way. The council admitted its responsibility. The grounds on which the residents failed were surreal. As we have seen in the chapter on Birmingham 2004 an election petition can only be brought by a candidate in the election, or a registered elector in the ward or constituency the election was for. Precisely because the petitioners had not been registered to vote – the very thing they were complaining about – they were unable to bring an election petition. (King op cit.)

There was one other attempt to bring an election petition. In the constituency of Birmingham Sparkbrook and Small Heath the Respect candidate Salma Yaqoob had gone from nowhere to twenty-seven per cent of the vote, reducing the majority for Labour's Roger Godsiff to only 3,289. The constituency included areas where Mr Justice Mawrey had found evidence of systematic, organised fraud only the year before. Salma Yaqoob's petition alleged that vulnerable voters had been pressured into voting a particular way and that applications for postal votes had been forged in the names of eligible voters, and that the return addresses given were those of the forgers not the voters – in short, very much the same sort of thing as had been found in the 2004 local elections, although it is important to note that no one alleged this had been done or condoned by Roger Godsiff himself, a man of integrity who had denounced the behaviour of Labour vote riggers the previous year.

The petition was never heard; legal aid was refused and Respect was unable to continue. As we have seen, in 2004 Labour's solicitors had lobbied hard to try to get their opponent's legal aid cut off – so hard that Mr Justice Mawrey himself intervened to persuade the authorities that continued support for the plaintiffs was in the public interest. Had he not done so that case might have been dropped and unelected fraudsters would have continued to "represent" the people of Birmingham with hardly anyone outside the area knowing or noticing the fact. It would be fascinating to know just who took the decision to discontinue legal aid in this case – and why?

In the run up to the 2005 General Election a headline in the Mail asked "Can We Trust This Election?" (Mail 06/04/05) . In many seats, almost certainly a substantial majority, the answer is still yes. In others it is a maybe at best. But unless safeguards are restored there is nothing to stop the numbers of the latter inexorably growing, while the former gradually melt away.

Am I My Brother's Cheater? Vote Rigging in Internal Party Elections

This chapter is about elections that differ in kind from the others covered in this book. The public as a whole do not get to vote in them. The winners do not *automatically* ascend to public office. (Indeed for at least one example we will look at, winning the internal party election proved to be a kiss of death in the subsequent public election.)

Rather than votes being cast aside or miscounted they are more likely to be devalued by "electoral colleges" that have been designed to produce a particular result. The examples in this chapter will all be drawn from the Labour Party. This does not mean that Labour is necessarily more dishonest than other parties but it has had internal elections for longer and perhaps the fact of its electoral dominance for the years from 1997 -2010 added extra bitterness to the struggle for spoils.

These elections are important for two reasons– in safe seats for one party or another they *can* precipitate the victor to public office, especially if the unfairness of the election was not widely known.

The second reason is that they are examples of utterly unscrupulous practice carried out in front of a watching world against people who are supposedly the party comrades of those doing it. We all need to ask the question "If these people are willing to do so much to frustrate the choices of the party members who are on their own side, how much more contempt must they feel for the votes of the rest of us?"

That said, there are those who do not appear to even register that there is anything wrong with this. In his witty and enlightening memoirs "Who Goes Home?" Roy Hattersley recounts how he was elected to the executive of the Socialist International's youth wing "Christopher Price took the proxies out of his pocket all of them provided by the phantom organisations which had headquarters (but, as far as I could make out, no members) in London. My triumph was secured when I received the support of the Azerbaijan Social Democrat Students in Exile." (p.13)

Probably the most famous example, certainly in England, was the contest to become Labour's first candidate for Mayor of London. Ever since the abolition of the GLC by Margaret Thatcher's Conservative government in the nineteen-eighties London had been the only capital city in the democratic world with no elected leader or authority of its own.

When New Labour came to power in 1997 they were pledged to change that. What the party's leaders never foresaw however was that that leader might be Ken Livingstone.

As leader of the GLC 'Red Ken' had been a hate figure for much of the press. Livingstone was a supporter of gay rights, racial equality and negotiations with Sinn Fein long before those things became fashionable. Nowadays they are government policy and part of the stated policy of every public body and most large companies. It takes an effort of will to recall that in the early eighties these views got you publically denounced with descriptions such as 'the IRA-loving, poof - loving Marxist leader of the GLC" (Sunday Express, 27/09/1981), "Commisar of County Hall" (Daily Mail 30/05/1981) "a dogmatic zealot" (Ibid) and "the most odious man in Britain" (Sun 13/10/1981). Granted, a combination of personal charm, the popular "Fares fair" policy and the ill-fated decision to abolish the GLC eventually helped swing public opinion back towards Livingstone and the GLC, nevertheless for most of Labour's modernisers and all of its old right 'Red Ken' was a walking symbol of the kind of 'extremism' they believed had cost Labour three General Elections. That he could actually be the popular choice didn't occur to any of them until it was too late.

Secondly, according to New Labour's worldview Ken Livingstone couldn't be the popular choice, regardless of evidence to the contrary. A key part of the New Labour project, the thing which had enabled Blair and his supporters to win over a vital section of the party and its supporters, was the belief that left wingers lost elections. This was more than an intellectual belief, it was an article of faith – without it what was the need or the excuse for New Labour at all? Nevertheless, from the moment the question was mooted Livingstone's support was strong in every poll taken and rising as time went on. As Livingstone's public support grew in the polls his internal party opponents were in the position of a man shouting

'"Don't all vote for him; can't you see he's unelectable?"' (Reasons To Be Cheerful, Mark Steel) Thus the Labour leadership set out to create a selection method for Labour candidate that Livingstone couldn't hope to win.

This method was to be the electoral college. In the electoral college the votes were divided into three sections, each to be decided by a different electorate. One third of the votes went to the party's London membership, voting individually. One third went to the London membership of those trades unions and other bodies (mainly the Co-op) that pay affiliation fees to the Labour party. One third went to London's Labour MPs, MEPs and candidates for the London Assembly.

The left wing Labour MP and lawyer Bob Marshall Andrews has said

"Few political labels are more likely to mislead the consumer than the "Electoral College". It has a subtle resonance calculated to promote confidence. It embraces and yokes together the spring of democracy (election) and the fire of intellectual integrity (college). It is a benign metaphor, civilised realpolitik. For precisely this reason it is almost always an instrument of political fraud." (Dragons Led By Poodles, Paul Flynn)

It is not necessary to agree completely to see that there are serious potential flaws in electoral college systems. The US President is elected by an electoral college that makes it possible, without any fraud or sharp practice required, for the candidate with fewest votes to be declared the winner.

It was repeatedly "spun" to the press that this was the same method used to elect Tony Blair as leader of the Labour Party. In fact, in two crucial aspects, it was not. Firstly, in the Labour leadership elections trades unionists voted as individuals. There was no room for a deal with union leaders to deliver the support of their members regardless of what those members wanted. In the selection contest for London mayoral candidate the decision on how to cast union members' votes was left to the discretion of full time officials. Worse, the RMT, Aslef and MSF unions were debarred from the voting in the trades union section on technical grounds, not long after their leaders had expressed support for Livingstone.

Secondly, only elected MPs and MEPs voted for Labour leader. In the London selectorate votes were also given to candidates – candidates who had all been vetted by a panel appointed by Labour's leadership to ensure their views were acceptable.

Because the section for MPs, MEPs and candidates accounted for a third of the total electorate each one of these hand-picked individuals had a vote counting for as much as 900 party members or 5,720 rank and file trades unionists. (Socialist Worker 13/11/1999) Dobson's support amongst this tiny group was reported in the Independent under the spectacularly misleading headline " Dobson gains Huge Lead over Livingstone." (Independent 28/10/1999)

A more sophisticated piece of spin claimed that rank and file members would decide the selection after all as the overwhelming support for Blair-backed Frank Dobson amongst candidates and MPs would cancel out Livingstone's huge support amongst trades unionists, leaving the party members as the key constituency. (Guardian 04/11/1999)

Looked at more closely of course this argument is an attempt to say that it is democratic, and acceptable, for a group of seventy-five people, fourteen of whom (the GLA candidates) were elected by and accountable to no one, to cancel out the votes of *hundreds of thousands* of trades unionists.

In the end it didn't work out like that at all. Not only did Livingstone win the support of every single trades union that balloted its members (In the firefighters union 97 per cent of votes cast) winning that section of the electoral college by 72 per cent to 28 per cent overall, he also won a substantial majority of individual members, 59.9 per cent to Frank Dobson's 40.1 per cent. Frank Dobson was then declared the winner, by 51.53 per cent to Livingstone's 48.47 per cent.

How was this possible?

The answer lies simply in the deliberate flaws in the system noted earlier. The AEEU decided to award the votes of its fifty thousand members to Frank Dobson without going to the trouble of balloting them. If they had balloted and come to the same result as every other union that would have won the selection for Livingstone. Much the same applies to the Co operative Wholesale Society (South London) Even without this the inclusion of the RMT, Aslef and the MSF would almost certainly have swung the electoral college. Not one of the GLA candidates backed Livingstone, as against a large majority of Labour members and an even larger majority of trades unionists. The candidates who would carry Labour's banner were thus exposed as being completely unrepresentative of both its membership and its core supporters.

The sequel is well known. Livingstone ran as an independent candidate and beat official Labour candidate Frank Dobson, an honest man widely believed to have been shoe horned into the whole mess by Downing Street pressure, into a humiliating third place with only 13.1 per cent of the vote. By any standards this was a painfully bad result for a governing party in its own capital city. A day or two later Jim Fitzpatrick MP was on a radio phone in justifying Labour's performance when the stand up comic Mark Steel, widely regarded as Britain's funniest Trotskyist, chipped in.

"Jimmy, it's Mark Steel here. We knew each other better when we were *both* members of the Socialist Workers Party. So how does it feel to be back where you started, as part of a tiny minority?" (Reasons To Be Cheerful, Mark Steel).

Really though, the shamed party managers had only themselves to blame. One of the marks of insanity is said to be expecting a different result from repeating the same behaviour and Labour had just undergone a near identical trauma in Wales.

Labour's route to self inflicted crucifixion west of the border began on October 26th 1998 when Ron Davies, Secretary of State for Wales, had a moment of madness on Clapham Common. For reasons which never became officially clear Mr Davies went for a late night walk on Clapham Common, ignoring two three line whips, where he met another man, a

Rastafarian and alleged procurer of women and boys with whom he instantly got on so well that they ended up going off together, picking up two other men from a south London block of flats and going on to a notorious estate "for a meal" whereupon said man robbed him. Mr Davies then contacted the Prime Minister and resigned.

This inherently strange and contradictory story was all over the papers the next day with immediate questions as to what the Secretary of State thought he was doing and why being robbed should be thought to be a resignation matter. It was almost universally assumed that Ron Davies had actually been seeking a homosexual encounter (for some reason no one questioned why that should be a resignation matter) to the astonishment of many of the MPs who thought they knew him best (Dragons Led By Poodles, Paul Flynn MP)

The hapless Ron Davies had been a political lynchpin – a politician well regarded by Downing Street but with majority support in all sections of the Welsh Labour movement. He had also been lined up to become Labour's first leader in the newly created National Assembly for Wales. His political demise left the obvious successor as the colourful Rhodri Morgan. This is where everything started to go pear shaped. In a decision widely believed to have been brought about by pressure from Labour's national leadership former Home Office minister and Ron Davies' replacement, newly appointed Secretary of State for Wales Alun Michael announced that he would run for the post of Labour's Welsh Assembly leader. It was a decision that would split the Labour Party in Wales and bring it to its worst ever electoral defeat.

It is still a mystery why Downing Street felt it necessary to try to deny Rhodri Morgan the leadership. Despite all the attempts to smear him during the campaign he was never what anyone could call a wild man. One of the reasons floated was the bizarre one that Rhodri Morgan's personal untidiness made the Prime Minister see him as unreliable provoking Roy Hattersley to write

"Nothing now surprises me about New Labour. So when I read that Tony Blair had been offended by the sight of Rhodri's untidy living room, I was quite prepared to believe that Alun is the Prime Minister's choice to lead the Welsh Assembly because he regularly props up the cushions on his sofa. " (Quoted in Flynn, op cit)

Perhaps it was as simple as the fact that Rhodri Morgan had a real, independent base of support meaning that he could become a centre of dissent if he chose. For all his talents, and even die hard Rhodri supporter Paul Flynn MP emphasises that they are very real it is hard to imagine Alun Michael being an independent centre of anything.

The electoral college, like that in London, was divided into a third of the vote each for Labour Party members voting individually, affiliated organisations (mainly trades unions but including the Co op and a few small socialist societies) and MPs, MEPs and candidates for the Welsh Assembly. Initially "candidates" included all those who had been adjudged as suitable candidates for the Assembly. Then "An opinion poll had found support for Rhodri among the unselected candidates running at three to one. So, a change was introduced by the Executive which disenfranchised all candidates who had not been selected for seats or for the regional lists." (Dragons Led By Poodles, Paul Flynn)

At a stroke this reduced Rhodri Morgan's potential vote, as selection for the "list" seats was "almost entirely in the hands of the party machine" (Flynn, op cit) a fact which saved the Alun Michael campaign from ignominious collapse when they found out that Alun Michael quite literally could not get himself selected for a constituency seat anywhere in Wales. Many of Labour's seats had already made their selections and the remainder appeared to show little enthusiasm for Mr Michael.

An attempt to gain the nomination for leader in Blaenau Gwent resulted in a three to one majority for Rhodri Morgan, despite Alun Michael having the backing of prominent figures, the local MP and the Co-op party

Despite the name the Co-op party is, like many trades unions, an affiliated body of the Labour Party with a say in internal contests, rather than a rival political organisation.

There is a long story behind this and anyone who wants to understand it should read the relevant chapter in "The Left: A Symposium" edited by

Gerald Kaufman. The Co-op party exists to promote the ideals of co-operativism and while most areas will have a Co-op party Blaenau Gwent is one of relatively few areas nowadays where it is still a significant force in the Labour movement. Alun Michael is a prominent member of the Co-op party. If he couldn't win the nomination from Blaenau Gwent, with the full backing of the local MP and where there were historical reasons for party members to resent Rhodri Morgan his chances of getting nominated for the actual seat, there or elsewhere did not look good.

Matters were compounded when Neath constituency Labour party (CLP) nominated Morgan as well. The MP for Neath was Peter Hain, once a prominent radical and anti-apartheid campaigner who was emerging as Alun Michael's most die hard supporter. (With his increasing willingness to defend the indefensible this campaign had already put Hain's feet on the path that would lead a few years later to touring the TV studios in the wake of the Birmingham vote rigging scandals denying that there was a problem.)

Alun Michael was forced to go for a "list" seat. List seats were the seats which would, under the Assembly's strange mix of first past the post and proportional representation, be used to "top up" parties' totals if the seats they won in the constituency section under-represented their share of the vote. Since Labour was expected to win the overwhelming majority of constituency seats it would be entitled to very few top up seats so to have a chance Alun Michael would have to head Labour's list, preferably in an area where Labour could count on strong support but not so strong they would win all the constituency seats. The Secretary of State was duly parachuted into Mid and West Wales while his supporter Professor Barry Jones of Cardiff University informed the world that this was purely because Alun Michael had not wanted to dislodge any constituency candidates, a claim which Newport MP Paul Flynn described as "Undiluted 100 per cent, copper-bottomed baloney" .(Flynn op cit.) The meeting where Alun Michael's candidacy was agreed was a stormy one with members voting down the platform's list of candidates four times due to the ruthlessness with which respected party members who happened to be admirers of Rhodri Morgan were excluded. (Flynn, op cit)

Worse, however, was to come. Peter Hain, who was running Alun Michael's campaign while ostensibly working full time as Minister of State at the Welsh Office sent out letters asking for support for his candidate using House of Commons (free) stationery, a clear breach of the rules. When challenged Hain's response was that they had accidentally been included with Christmas cards sent out by his office. Unfortunately Christmas cards are not allowed to be sent using Commons pre-franked envelopes either.

As misdemeanours go this one probably had little or no effect on the election's outcome. The same could not be said for the way in which the union votes were cast.

Unison, to its credit, decided to hold a ballot of its members and vote accordingly. The results gave Rhodri Morgan 74 per cent of the vote with a lead of around five thousand individual votes. Peter Hain promptly claimed that this was because Unison in Wales was full of Trotskyists. Quite apart from the fact that Rhodri Morgan is not and never has been a Trotskyist and certainly couldn't count on Trotskyist votes this is simply untrue. There are not more than a few thousand organised Trotskyists in the whole of Britain and the idea that they had all somehow managed to join the Welsh section of Unison is untenable. As Mark Steel gleefully pointed out "Wouldn't someone have noticed if there were 5,000 Trotskyists in Welsh Unison? Anyone arriving in casualty at Swansea General Hospital would be treated to a lecture about petty bourgeois vacillations. It would be impossible to walk across a park in Abergavenny without bumping into council gardeners giving out leaflets denouncing each other." (Mark Steel, op cit) Those with long memories will recall that Peter Hain is the author of a book called "The Democratic Alternative" published in 1983 in which he argued that democracy faced increasing erosion in Britain. At the time this was taken as a warning – looking at Hain's role in this election raises the disturbing possibility that it was a statement of intent.

Most Welsh unions however, decided not to follow Unison's procedure. The Transport and General Workers Union, for example, with 5.1 per cent of the *total* vote for leader decided to simply give it all to Alun Michael. The T & G Welsh secretary (described by one Labour MP as a Gauleiter) George Wright, was noted for his kneejerk loyalty towards

Labour leaders . Sadly this had led to him bitterly attacking Neil Kinnock in the late nineteen seventies when Kinnock publically opposed party policy on Welsh devolution. When Kinnock then became the next Labour leader but one Wright's influence went into a noticeable decline. (Flynn, op cit & "The Making of Neil Kinnock" by Robert Harris).

The current affairs programme Dispatches commissioned a poll of Wright's members, with the help of Harris Research and the Electoral Reform Society which showed that they would opt for Rhodri Morgan by 70 per cent to 30 per cent.

George Wright replied "we're backing the Secretary of State because he's the Secretary of State...If Rhodri was the Secretary of State for Wales we'd back him." (quoted in Flynn, op cit). Whether his members felt the same waywas a question he seemed disinclined to consider but he did at least have the courage to defend himself publically.

One branch official of the ISTC, the steelworkers union, whose members were not balloted before the leadership decided to give their votes to Alun Michael finally tracked down a record of this decision on page 195 of an internal union report. It simply read

"With the General Secretary now in the House of Lords the Confederation (ISTC) will have political representation at all levels. With regard to the election of the Leader of the Welsh Assembly it had been decided to support Mr Alun Michael MP."

"Who decided?" the member not unreasonably wondered to his MP. "And is there any significance in the juxtaposition of those two sentences?" (Flynn, op cit)

The AEEU (covering engineering workers, electricians and plumbers) with 6.2 per cent of the total vote took the decision via a delegate conference. The Morgan camp accused Peter Hain of having a list of delegates which he was using to lobby them on Alun Michael's behalf. Hain described this as "smears and ridiculous allegations which are groundless"

Clearly not groundless however was the letter to Wales on Sunday from a member of the AEEU revealing that the 4,000 strong Swansea branch was unrepresented at the delegate conference, (Flynn, op cit) a fact which cannot help but raise the question of just how representative it actually was. The conference voted overwhelmingly for Alun Michael. Either engineering workers think very differently from those in health, transport, firefighting, mining and local government or the conference was not representative. In the absence of a democratic ballot it is, at this stage, impossible to say.

The GMB (General and Municipal Workers, Boilermakers and Allied Trades) avoided criticism of their methods of deciding how to cast their members' 6.2 per cent of the vote by not telling anyone what it was. There *were* indicative ballots held in some (not all) branches but these went largely to Rhodri Morgan. The union gave all its votes to Alun Michael. To this day the details of how this decision was reached have not been disclosed. A GMB member wrote to Paul Flynn MP alleging ballot rigging. (Flynn, op cit) Without far more evidence than is available it would be wholly wrong to suggest such a thing. In any case, since the GMB leadership cast its vote without having to take ballots into account what would be the point?

Similar patterns were repeated in many other unions. To be fair it was by no means all one sided – several unions cast their votes for Rhodri Morgan without holding a ballot of the membership. What is undeniable though is that in every single trades union that held a One Member One Vote ballot, Unison, the FBU, MSF and the NUM the membership voted overwhelmingly for Rhodri Morgan. A week or so before the election a rumour that the overall electoral college result would be 65 per cent for Alun Michael and 35 per cent for Rhodri Morgan began circulating. Disturbingly, on February 20th this turned out to be absolutely correct – despite the fact that Morgan won 64 per cent of all members votes and an even higher percentage of votes in all unions that balloted their members. Alun Michael now faced the daunting prospect of leading an election campaign in a country that showed every sign of wanting to vote for somebody else. A Welsh newspaper commented that "This is a sad day for Welsh democracy....Perhaps the happiest man is Daffyd Wigley [leader of Plaid Cymru, the Welsh nationalist party S.B.]

Tony Blair allegedly responded "The Welsh must put aside their dark, despairing Celtic side" (Flynn, op cit). The events of the near future would leave plenty of despair in the hearts of Welsh Labour. For avowedly Celtic Plaid Cymru however Christmas was about to come early.

Rhodri Morgan and his supporters, meanwhile, faced the question of how exactly his opponents had known the result beforehand? The ballot had been conducted by USB, a firm set up by the trades unions to conduct internal ballots following alleged irregularities and coincidentally had been criticised the year before when advance rumours of the election results for Labour's National Executive also turned out to be uncannily accurate. The ubiquitous Paul Flynn MP who had acted as an international election observer in Bulgaria considered USB's operating methods to be "less than professional and open to tampering". (Flynn, op cit). Rhodri Morgan wrote and complained and was answered with a brief letter from USB stating their confidence that the ballot was carried out "secretly and fairly" and an anonymous quote to the press calling him a "whinger" and claiming that Labour's members "don't want to waste time over an election which everyone accepts had one winner." (Flynn, op cit) Everyone, of course, accepted no such thing, which doubtless accounts for the vehemence of the response.

It was at this point that a little cloud, no larger than a man's hand started to tower into an ominous cumulo-nimbus. There had been such a controversial contest for the post of Labour's candidate for leader of the Welsh Assembly that most observers seemed to have forgotten that to actually become leader the candidate had to have a majority *in* the Assembly. There were excellent reasons for this carelessness. South Wales is Labour's heartland like almost nowhere else and seventy per cent of the Welsh population are concentrated in the south. Built on a solid foundation of coal, steel and engineering Labour's seats in the valleys are the stuff of socialist legend, land of Nye Bevan, Michael Foot, the Chartist risings. Even in the darkest days of the eighties Labour could count on Welsh majorities that were literally unassailable. The Tories, even in a good year, were confined to a few pockets of affluence in rural and suburban areas, the nationalists largely to the Welsh speaking north and west.   Even the introduction of a semi-proportional electoral system shouldn't have changed that because Labour's electoral dominance was based on real support, not a trick of a split opposition in a first past the post system as for so many parties in so many seats.

Within a few weeks of the results of Labour's internal contest it was fighting a real election for the Welsh Assembly. Twenty four hours before that election's results were announced Peter Hain said they were going to be "a major triumph for the Labour Party....Plaid will have to examine its political ethos after this election. It's going to be the death of Old Nationalism."

When the results from the May 6th 1999 Assembly elections were announced they were the worst that Labour had ever suffered anywhere in any region or nation of the UK in the whole of its history. The beneficiary was Plaid Cymru. The swing away from Labour was greater than that to Labour in 1945 or 1997, greater than that to the Conservatives in 1979 and 1983, greater than in any British election since the vote had been won by ordinary men and women.

Labour lost Islwyn, formerly the seat of Labour leader Neil Kinnock, it lost the Rhondda, the second safest seat in the UK. The Rhondda is so traditionally left wing that the only previous occasion Labour was run close there was in 1945 by Communist leader Harry Pollitt. It lost the formerly rock-solid Llanelli.

Labour pundits on telly to discuss the election result sat dumbfounded "Media junkies train themselves beforehand to cope with every plausible eventuality... They had not practiced for the End of the World." (Flynn, op cit) Labour lost the majority in the Assembly. Alun Morgan's career entered a political black hole and Rhodri Morgan went on to become a popular and successful First Minister of Wales.

Paul Flynn MP remarked that not every election can be stitched. Only two years after the Assembly elections of course the legislation on postal voting came into force that would lead to unscrupulous men and women from all parties trying to do exactly that.

One more example. In the spring of 2009 the selection contest to become Labour's candidate for the Labour seat of Erith and Thamesmead, an outer London constituency containing both moderately affluent suburbs and small towns and some of the poorest and ugliest council estates anywhere took place. The area contains or is near the sites of several well known racial murders and saw demonstrations both for and against the fascist right in the early nineteen nineties.

For reasons which doubtless seemed good at the time a number of Labour's leading figures including Cabinet Minister Tessa Jowell and Blair's former right hand man, Alistair Campbell decided that the ideal candidate for this area was a twenty-two year old Oxford graduate whose main work experience had been as a part-timer for Tony Blair's Faith Foundation and who was still studying at the LSE.

The fact that she was Georgia Gould, daughter of Lord Phillip Gould doubtless did not influence them in any way. Phillip Gould, for the uninitiated, is a personal friend of Peter Mandelson and Alistair Campbell, a former Labour Party HQ staffer, polling and strategy adviser to Labour for five successive General Elections and all round New Labour insider who was made a peer in 2004 by the New Labour government. His daughter Georgia has been involved in politics almost since she was born – at least, she appeared on the front of a Labour policy statement as a small child. Cabinet Minister Tessa Jowell broke parliamentary convention by choosing to speak in Ms Gould's support in the constituency without bothering to inform the retiring local MP John Austin.

So far, so what? After all, nepotism isn't the same thing as ballot rigging by any means – even when the fact of a candidate's wealthy, well-connected family background gives them the means to distribute a glossy brochure to the electorate and have Cabinet Ministers come to speak in their support. However, reports of more than simple favouritism were by now emanating from the constituency.

At least a third of Labour members were reportedly registered to vote by post. This in itself raises questions – the rules for postal voting in Labour selection contests are very similar to what they used to be for public elections before the Representation of the People Act 2000. Postal votes are supposed to be given only to those who cannot attend hustings, not "on demand".

Seventy one year old Labour member Barbara Cooley told political weekly Tribune that two individuals had come knocking on her door with a completed postal ballot application form which they persuaded her to sign, even though she said she would be attending the hustings. They subsequently turned out to be Gould supporters (Guardian 18/04/2009), (Tribune 20/04/2009)

Twenty one year old Labour member and student Mohammed Iqbal had a similar experience. Mr Iqbal told the Guardian that " a Gould supporter visited him on 28th March with a postal vote application form already filled in with his name and address 'The part where you put a valid reason for requesting the postal vote was crossed out,' he said. "She told me that the party had changed its policy and that everyone would be receiving ballot papers in advance and this was how to register for one'...Two weeks later Iqbal says he received a confirmation that his postal vote application had been accepted 'I still thought it was strange because I hadn't given a reason to ask for a postal vote and I had told this woman I was going to the hustings so I rang up to speak to someone about it. The man on the phone told me the reason I had given for not being able to attend was 'university course deadline'. But I hadn't filled in that bit on the form." (Guardian 25/04/2009)

It is unclear who Mr Iqbal would have spoken to because for reasons unknown the selection process in Erith & Thamesmead was taken out of the hands of the local party. The sitting MP asked Labour's General Secretary for an investigation, so far without success.

(A cynic might wonder if the selection had been taken out of the hands of the local party because of the events of Labour's national conference in 2005. As is well known an octogenarian delegate, Walter Wolfgang was forcibly removed from the hall for shouting "Nonsense" at Cabinet Minister Jack Straw and then prevented from re-entering the hall by police officers using powers granted them under the Terrorism Act 2000. Less well known is that another delegate was also thrown out for attempting to intervene on his behalf. That delegate was Steve Forrest, Chair of Erith & Thamesmead Constituency Labour party.)

Furthermore this news brought calls for an investigation into the West Yorkshire seat of Calder Valley where Cherie Blair's stepmother lost the hustings to local mayor Susan Press but was declared to be the selected candidate due to postal votes, despite allegations that canvassers had helped voters to fill in their postal voting forms, a clear breach of the rules. Local party secretary Paul Clarke wrote to regional party officials asking for an investigation. (Telegraph 15/04/2009). As with Erith & Thamesmead so far no result has been forthcoming.

All this however pales beside what was to come. The night before the hustings the whole process was put on hold when it was revealed that a ballot box containing postal votes which was being stored in a locked room at London Labour Party HQ had been broken into and some of the ballots destroyed. (Guardian 18/04/2009)

Speculation ran rife. Ms Gould herself sent an email to her supporters which appeared to blame the hard left. On the face of it this seems unlikely since the last time the hard left had access to Labour's HQ was around about the time she was born. (Telegraph 18/04/2009 Labour ballot box tampering row deepens)

Without more evidence either way any speculations are worthless at best and slanderous at worst. The police were asked to investigate but declined – as the election is not a public one they have no powers – even though the effect could have been similar to rigging a public election if the ballot destruction had slipped by unnoticed.

The ballot was re-run, Ms Gould failed to win the candidacy and no explanation for who accessed and destroyed ballots and in whose interests has ever emerged. Although a fingerprint was allegedly found on the torn-up ballot papers an internal party enquiry was abandoned apparently because of fears that asking staff for their fingerprints might violate their human rights. (Guardian 29/09/2010, Labour party abandons ballot tampering inquiry)

The fact of ballot tampering makes one thing certain though. Someone in the highest ranks of one of Britain's three governmental parties has no scruples whatsoever. And as we asked earlier, if they have no scruples about destroying the votes of their own party comrades how likely are they to care about the votes of the public?

E-voting, E-counting, EDS and other tales of an ordinary madness

E voting and e counting contrary to what many might think are any form of electronic voting or counting of votes – they do not necessarily involve the internet. They may include methods whereby the voter will mark a physical ballot paper by hand and then the votes be counted electronically by a scanner or some other such device.

Alternatively the voter may use some form of computer to print off a paper ballot, or the whole process may be electronic with a vote being cast electronically and perhaps remotely to be registered by an IT system.

E voting and e counting of whatever sort has a history of vulnerability to fraud or to system failure as the United States and the Netherlands, where its use is widespread, have cause to know. It has also been used in a number of Second and Third world countries most of which have, such is the nature of the international e-voting trade, bought their systems wholesale from the same small group of US based companies. There is only one country in the world that has experimented with a standard nationwide e-voting DRE system. That country is Brazil and there was near immediate scandal. The electronic voting system had been introduced for votes by Senators as well as for public elections. In connection with the impeachment of a corrupt Senator it was revealed that it was possible to cast electronic votes for Senators in their absence – and without their knowledge or consent. A paper trail for the 2002 Presidential elections had to be introduced amid widespread popular unrest.

On the night of the election the votes for Lula Da Silva of the Workers' Party suddenly dropped from more than a million to *minus* forty one thousand. The system was rebooted and Lula went on to win the election after a second round but to this day many Brazilians believe that foul play was involved. (Steal This Vote, Andrew Gumbel, 2005).

In the US in 1985 in the Dallas mayoral elections the incumbent, Starke Taylor was trailing opposition candidate Max Goldblatt when the computer processing the votes crashed. When it came up again he was inexplicably in the lead and stayed that way aided and abetted by mysterious incidents in which votes already recorded for his opponent would vanish while the number of votes actually recorded as being cast shot up and down like a skyrocket.

Outraged, Goldblatt and his election manager took the whole thing to court only to discover that there was effectively no paper trail, most records already having been destroyed.

In the absence of any proof of fraud or error the Goldblatt team were unable to prove their case but enough bad publicity was generated to trigger a public outcry and investigation at the end of which the Attorney General's office concluded, in language which Mawrey would have recognised

"..the electronic voting system in use lacks adequate security features to provide any assurances of the absence of fraud...As a result, this office has found that it will be difficult to demonstrate..that Texas elections are free from fraud.." (quoted in Gumbel, op cit)

Similar things have happened in Mexican Presidential elections with the difference that many people who will think the worst of elections in Third World countries are all too likely to assume the integrity of elections in prosperous, powerful nations with a long democratic history.

In Riverside County, California in 2000 where a touch screen electronic voting system had just been introduced (Direct Recording Electronic voting machines, known as DREs)

"the tabulation software overloaded and started deleting votes from the tallying system instead of adding them. Sequoia [the company that provided the voting machines and software SB] had to send in an emergency resuscitation team, creating a delay of several hours." (Gumbel op cit)

In itself this might have been no more than a harmless glitch but as in Dallas fifteen years before a candidate who had been ahead when the system went down was behind when it came up again.

The response of county registrar Mischelle [sic SB] Townsend was to describe the election's running as "flawless". The flawlessness of Riverside's new system was widely reported. The problems were not. This prompted a large number of counties determined never again to risk a 'hanging chad' election like the bitterly disputed 2000 Presidential contest to invest in the new electronic voting and counting machines. According to Time magazine fifty thousand touch screen machines were bought across thirty seven states. (Time 03/11/2007) What doesn't seem to have occurred to any of the states at the time was that DREs made recounts impossible. None of them seem to have known that academic experts from institutions as prestigious as Stanford and Harvard had criticised DRE systems as inherently insecure.

None of them knew at the time that software for Diebold, the main seller of DREs would be stolen and that with that an election result could be altered anywhere a Diebold machine was in use – and altered undetectably. Some observers were to be intensely suspicious at the results of the 2002 elections in Georgia in which there were double digit voting swings which the opinion polls had failed to pick up at all. (Gumbel, op. cit). Diebold say they have updated their software since the theft and thus there is no cause for alarm

In 2004 the Cabinet Office issued a briefing entitled "e voting standards for UK elections" under the aegis of John Borras, Director of Technology to the Office of the e-Envoy. The first aim it lists is

"An e-enabled General Election some time after 2006"

It goes on to add "remote unsupervised voting" to its list – in the form I have it available it seems to have been designed as a presentation to a meeting (Http://xml.coverpages.org/BorrasUK/evoting.pdf) which would perhaps explain the lack of complete sentences and the huge amounts it leaves unexplained. "Critical Success Factors" in e voting in the UK include the bullet points

"- Making voting more straightforward for the public and more aligned to everyday life

- Making elections more accessible, more attractive and more convenient

- Maintaining public confidence in the security of the systems

- Improving the efficiency and effectiveness of electoral administration

- Contain costs "

It is not the fault of John Borras, or whoever drew this up but this modest list of objectives was always likely to be in trouble before it started. Nor is it the fault of John Borras that his earlier objective "remote unsupervised voting" directly contradicts the bullet point above "Maintaining public confidence in the security of the systems." Remote voting is insecure by definition and always will be because there is no way of knowing if that vote was cast in secrecy or under coercion.

As for containing costs and improving efficiency and effectiveness , well, any e voting system will require the purchase of new hardware and a new IT system. IT systems were New Labour's most consistent failure. From the day it came to power the government was a ridiculously easy mark for every snake oil salesman with a failed IT system to offload. Time overruns, cost overruns and failure to function properly have hit basic government operations again and again until books can and have been filled with them. The Home Office, Customs & Excise, the Inland Revenue, the NHS, the Child Support Agency and the Immigration and Nationality Department have all been hit. (Plundering the Public Sector, David Craig, 2006 pp1-11)

To take just one example the Child Support Agency bought a system from EDS. The system was due to go live in October 2001 but didn't actually start running until March 2003. This might have been justifiable, if no great advert for the firm, provided the delays had been used to sort out problems with the system. Unfortunately, a year after that the system had increased the cost of processing an application by a fifth, staff were in despair and the average time it took for maintenance payments to be set up had risen to twenty-two weeks. On top of this the system was millions over budget. (Craig, op cit) Given this, hopes of a cheap effective system for elections seemed exaggerated.

Pilots of e-counting took place in 2007 in six different councils, Bedford, South Buckinghamshire, Dover, Breckland, Warwick and Stratford upon Avon. At South Bucks an e-voting and e-counting pilot took place. These took place against the publically stated opposition of the Chair of the Committee on Standards in Public Life, Sir Alastair Graham, who told the conference of the Association of Electoral Administrators

"How does the DCA or the Electoral Commission know about the extent of electoral fraud when neither of them have kept any statistics nor have undertaken any research on the issue? Is it that, in their obsession with increasing participation at all costs, they have turned a blind eye to the risks of electoral fraud and its consequences on the integrity of our democratic system....It is a matter of serious concern that we are experimenting with insecure methods of voting when the current registration and absent voting procedures are so insecure." (Quoted in the ORG report on the 2007 pilots)

There were also 'repeat pilots' in Swindon, Rushmoor, Bedford, Shrewsbury and Sheffield which had experimented with alternative voting systems in the past.

Ominously the e-voting in South Bucks was run by Election Systems & Software (ES &S). Although the name means little to British voters clued up Americans might recognise it and clued up Venezuelan or Filipino voters certainly would. ES & S was once purveyor of the Votomatic punch card voting machine which was used for many years in elections across the US, despite the fact that their rivals, armed with a doctored punch card and a thumb tack, demonstrated on the floor of Congress just how easy elections held with the Votomatic were to rig.

Unfortunately most people at the time thought it was a simple case of commercial jealousy. They may well have been right but overlooked the fact that all the allegations were still true. E S & S was glad to dump the Votomatic and move to DRE voting but still continued to suffer from what was clearly either painful incompetence or extraordinary bad luck. Venezualans will not quickly forget that their 2000 Presidential election had to be postponed because E S & S's software simply wasn't up to the task. (Gumbel op cit) E S & S claimed that the Venezualans had simply made too many changes of detail in their election at the last minute. Oddly enough this is the same excuse used by IT companies when the systems they sell to the British government fail to work (Craig op cit)

Similar problems on a smaller scale dogged its operations in the Phillipines.

In the USA ES & S had been responsible for the computerised voting machines that in 2002 Primary elections had shown a nine hundred per cent turnout in one precinct . An examination of Es & S's iVotronic voting machine sponsored by the Florida Department of State and conducted in a lab reported specific vulnerabilities which laid the machines open to potential manipulation.

In the Netherlands e-voting was abandoned altogether after the group "Wij vertrouwen stemcomputers niet" (We do not trust voting machines) demonstrated that Nedap voting machines could not only be easily and undetectably hacked but with simple electronic devices anyone standing within forty feet of the machine at the time could tell how someone voted. Voting in the Netherlands is now done exclusively using paper and pencil. Bizarrely, the State of New York is reported to be considering buying 28,000 Nedap machines. (See Wij vertrouwen website)

Returning to the 2007 UK pilots, in three of them, Stratford, Breckland and Warwick , the pilot failed so spectacularly that the votes actually had to be counted by hand. In addition "All counts took longer to undertake than had been envisaged prior to the elections.

Only the count at Dover was quicker than a previous manual count. "(Electoral Commission Report- May 2007 electoral pilot schemes.). Considering that speed was supposed to be a feature of e-counting this was less than good news. This may, of course have had something to do with the large number of votes that had to be checked by hand as "a higher than expected number of ballots were sent for adjudication" (Electoral Commision report). As for containing costs the Electoral Commission's report states

"The additional costs associated with e-counting varied from about £1.50 to £2.00 per elector" – not a huge sum but definitely one that needs justifying by improved results. As the commission's report said, these pilots "did not contribute greatly to learning how the efficiency of e-counting solutions can be maximised although they have highlighted instances of poor practice."

One instance of poor practice highlighted was that at South Bucks the council put themselves almost entirely into the hands of ES & S. Without wishing in any way to impugn the company's integrity it is simply not appropriate for a democratic election to be handed over to a private company whose primary concerns are going to be increasing profitability. In addition there is always going to be a powerful motive for a company that lives by selling election technology to conceal any potential flaws or breaches in its system as far as possible. South Bucks' given reason for holding the pilot is also interesting. They said that it was "impossible" to continue voting in the old way because of their difficulties recruiting staff. This is clearly untrue. Elections have been run in the old way for more than a century. It is simply beyond belief that the available labour pool should mysteriously vanish for no apparent reason at the exact moment that electronic voting becomes a legal and technical possibility.

In the 2007 pilots there were observers from not only the Electoral Commision but from the Open Rights Group. A group of IT professionals and academics, ORG initially concerned itself with digital copyright issues but in recent years has become more and more concerned with the integrity of e-enabled elections. Their report makes detailed and fascinating reading.

It states "The e-voting and e-counting technologies deployed on this occasion did not conform to the standards expected by Returning Officers (ROs) and their agents. Inadequate attention was given to system design, systems access and audit trails. Systems used both inappropriate hardware and software and were insufficiently secured. Problems included: use of desktop productivity software, machines in public areas with open ports, informal transfer of files using personal devices, and single-factor authentication." (Open Rights Group May 2007 Election Report)

At Rushmoor the Labour party candidate logged on to find the Labour logo by his Conservative opponent's name and the system blocking him from voting – a problem which, as it was blatantly obvious, was swiftly dealt with but leaves one wondering if other less obvious problems with the recording of e votes might have been present. (ORG op cit)

Also at Rushmoor computer terminals in the public libraries had been designated for internet voting purposes. An ORG observer found that at least two of them had open USB ports which left them wide open for potential attack with software that could either manipulate votes or find out who was voting for whom.

At Sheffield numbers of voters reported being unable to vote online at all. An OPT2VOTE representative confirmed that this was the case and was due to a software problem. In Swindon laptops at the polling places provided for voters to use were often placed so that screens were in full view of anyone in the room, seriously undermining the secrecy of the ballot.

At Breckland District Council in Norfolk the counting of the ballot was soon to descend into a frightening farce. The counting was initially very slow due to scanner problems, but this in itself was no threat to the integrity of the election process. What was, and immediately, was the repeated discovery of ballots for one ward in the boxes for another.

As we saw back in chapter two, ballot boxes are physically sealed and brought in to the counting process under guard by election officials all the way. The seals are not to be broken until time for counting to begin. If this procedure was followed it is impossible to see how or why ballot boxes *could* contain ballots from another ward – unless voters were perversely placing their ballots in the wrong boxes in the first place or votes were being examined and then placed *back inside* the ballot boxes. No explanation was offered.

When, as was frequently the case, the scanners failed to read the barcodes on ballots staff were instructed to enter the barcode numbers by hand. A Mr Timothy Birt, election agent for the Green Party and clearly a man who knows his way around a computer had asked the e-counting suppliers, Indra, whether there was a checksum digit in operation. A checksum digit, in simple terms, is a mechanism preventing incorrect numbers from being registered or the same numbers being counted twice. Out of interest Mr Birt persuaded a poll worker to enter an incorrect barcode number. It was accepted: either there was no checksum digit or it didn't work –at a stroke the results became less trustworthy.

Shortly after this Mr Birt, observing an adjudication screen saw two ballots which had been scanned as one and asked for them to be set aside for further adjudication

by the Returning Officer. When the time came for the result of that particular ward to be announced Mr Birt enquired how the RO had resolved the issue. The RO had never heard of the issue and wanted to go ahead and declare since one vote wouldn't make a difference, but on Mr Birt's insistence offered to add the extra ballot "manually". This caused Birt some considerable concern as he felt that if votes could be added manually it called the existing security checks into immediate question.

Little did he know the night's worries were just beginning. There were elections for a town council as well as Brecklands District Council taking place on the same day, being counted on the same night and with voting having taken place in the same polling stations.

Consequently the hyperactive Mr Birt and others were concerned when the e-counting gave a turnout for the Dereham-Humbletoft ward in the district elections as only 13.91 per cent, while the turnout for the town council election in the same seat was 31.55 per cent. Since voters had been handed their ballot papers for the elections together this result was only possible if more than half of all voters had thrown away or taken home their ballot papers for the district council elections, while voting assiduously for the much less powerful or important town council. On the face of it this seemed unlikely.

A manual recount showed that it was completely wrong. Several hundred votes had not been counted, which when counted brought turnouts to an almost identical level. *This was the only ward in the country where votes were*

counted both electronically and manually and 56.1 per cent of votes had been missed by e-counting. In addition, one of the votes found was from the neighbouring Dereham-Central ward – its barcode indicated that it had already been counted. How it got there no one could say. Dereham-Central was showing similar discrepancies albeit the other way round with a district election turnout registered as 32.34 per cent and a town council turnout of only 15.86 per cent. Despite this being pointed out the RO did not order a recount.

Due to the intensely slow pace of counting, all concerned – candidates, agents and election staff – eventually agreed to leave the count uncompleted and convene the following Monday morning at Brecklands Council's offices to complete the count manually.

In the light of what had happened with Dereham-Humbletoft there were several requests for the already declared electronically counted wards to be re-counted. The Returning Officer refused. Nor would he accept the Green Party's requests that there be no formal declarations until all the wards had been counted for fear that ballots for different wards might have become mixed. In a display of impressive bravado the RO stated his 'total confidence' that there had been no cross contamination. It was at this time that the Green Party and several other party representatives present formally announced that they had lost confidence in the Returning Officer.(ORG op cit). Sadly for the RO "Throughout the day ballot papers from the wrong wards were discovered in ballot boxes. Often the ballots were for wards already declared." (ORG op cit)

Understandably given the evidence Mr Birt and many others, reportedly including Breckland council's group of Labour councillors, continued to have serious doubts about the validity of the results. Consequently the ever vigilant Mr Birt and a colleague, Mr Alan Osborn got permission to inspect the marked register for two wards,Thetford Castle and Two Rivers.

In Thetford Castle there were six ballot papers fewer than there should have been. In Two Rivers ward there were two hundred and twenty-one *more* than there should have been. Words are inadequate. Casting our minds back to the description of how traditional British elections work in chapter two, the first line of defence at the count is the check that the same number of ballot papers are coming out of the ballot box as went into it. A discrepancy of a handful of votes, less than five, say, might be a mistake. A discrepancy of two hundred and twenty one ought to have got the election for that ward called to an immediate halt.

There is no possible legitimate way for that number of votes to have gone unrecorded. It is very hard to think of any way it could have happened even through the grossest of incompetence. The implication has to be deliberate fraud by persons unknown and due to the e-counting system it had gone completely unnoticed until the 22nd of May – not enough time left before the twenty one day deadline to organise an election petition, even if the Green party had had the money. The Breckland Green party has since called for an independent public enquiry.

The Open Rights Group used a Freedom of Information request to obtain audit logs of the e-counting process from Breckland District Council. After examining them they concluded "actions do not match within the logs...There appears to be an insufficient level of detail in the log for meaningful analysis or verification of the count process. Finally ORG has been given no method by which to verify the accuracy and integrity of the log files provided." (ORG op cit)

Breckland was not the only place where this was going on. In South Bucks nothing was produced to show that the number of ballots counted matched those issued. In Bedford the Returning Officer "was willing to ignore discrepancies of up to a hundred votes." (ORG op cit)

Possibly this had something to do with the fact that at the Bedford count "it became clear that the same ballot papers were being adjudicated repeatedly without the decisions being saved" (ORG op cit) thus opening the possibility of double counting. In Bedford, counting was still going on at 10.20 pm on the day after the election when representatives of the three main parties approached the Returning Officer to tell him that they were losing confidence and to request a manual count of the remaining votes the next working day (which since it was already Friday night and there was a Bank Holiday coming up would have been the following Tuesday.)

The RO refused on two grounds, firstly that this would undermine confidence in the votes already declared and secondly that he had been assured by the supplier, Indra, that votes could not be double counted.

The RO had no way, of course, of knowing that Indra's count at Brecklands was already fast descending into chaos, nor that Indra had "assured" Mr Birt that they were using a checksum digit safeguard and been proved wrong. The first reason given however is utterly illogical (The RO must have been very tired and under tremendous pressure at the time) If a count is unreliable it deserves to have confidence in it undermined.

Within the next forty minutes it was observed that the number of ballots showing as waiting for second level adjudication began to fall *even though no staff were logged in to the second level adjudication system.*

In response to further complaints the RO told those present "You don't get a recount on an electronic system." This might be true of e-voting: it is one of the most powerful arguments against it. It is only true of e-counting if the Returning Officer chooses to make it so.

The RO also told complainants that "Breckland got the same answer on a manual recount." We know this is untrue. It would be very interesting to know who told this falsehood to the Returning Officer and why.

Eventually the final results in the Bedford elections were announced at 1.36 am, the RO brushing aside further requests for recounts. The whole process had taken more than fifteen and a half hours.

In Stratford ballots were also having to be frequently rescanned – in addition candidates and observers felt they had no real way of scrutinising the process, the operators' screens and scanners being turned away from view and protected by barriers of tables. A local Conservative compared the experience to staring at the back of a TV with the sound turned off. (ORG op cit) The Returning Officer ordered a report to be written into the conduct of the election.

In several places traditional metal ballot boxes had been replaced by flatpacks constructed out of corrugated plastic and with a wide slot. Candidates, agents and observers were all concerned that these might be much more vulnerable to ballot stuffing than the usual narrow slotted metal boxes. Given that the checks on the number of votes coming out of the ballot boxes were being abandoned or ignored in several areas that night this fear is a serious one. It would crop up again in other elections later.

The ORG report also states "How and when electronic vote tallies combined with other subtotals was, in all observed areas, a mysterious process, not open to observation or verification. ..Electors cast their votes and ROs declared results; whatever occurred in the time between those actions was hidden from view by the technologies and processes used. In South Bucks and Swindon votes were downloaded and counted on computers controlled by suppliers' staff without any

candidate, agent or observer able to examine the process. What could actually have been seen on the computer screens is itself questionable, but the very fact that this was not allowed to be observed was an unacceptable restriction on the count process." (ORG op cit) Matters in South Bucks were not helped by the fact that ES&S staff had been forbidden to speak to observers.

"The amount of information provided to candidates and their agents was wholly insufficient for them to be able to verify in any meaningful sense that the results were accurate before accepting their declaration...ORG is unable to rule out either [error or fraud] due to its inability to observe any of the crucial parts of the e-voting elections conducted."

They did observe that there were known vulnerabilities in some of the software used and warned that internet voting was doubly vulnerable "Because of the Internet's global nature and the low cost of access the potential for attacks from anywhere in the world are considerable." ORG op cit)

ORG observers being mostly software experts, might, with enough access, access that the suppliers of voting technology have always been very reluctant to grant, have been able to tell if the e-voting totals were correct, although even that is not certain.

Ordinary people, including candidates and their agents could not. If e-voting were to spread we would, like the citizens of some Bronze Age theocracy, be unable to run our affairs without trusting the word of a small band of elite experts who we would be wholly unqualified to challenge.

The ORG concluded that they could not express confidence in the election results declared in the areas they observed. The danger is that if e-voting and e-counting spread we will never again be able to express confidence in any election result. We will just have to take our rulers' word for it.

One Step Forward? The Electoral Administration Act OF 2006

After the 2005 General Election the newly re-elected government started looking at electoral fraud as an issue and came up with the Electoral Administration Act which received Royal Assent (and thus became law) on 11/07/2006.

The explanatory notes to the Act which can be found online here (www.opsi.gov.uk) state that the object of the Act is to respond to the Electoral Commission reports *Voting for change* (June 2003) , *Delivering Democracy? The future of postal voting* (December 2004) and *Securing the vote* (May 2005). The notes also state

"7.   Following the Birmingham elections court case (2005) and allegations of fraud at the May 2005 General Election, none of which have resulted to date in prosecution, the Government undertook policy discussions with its stakeholders on a range of proposals aimed at safeguarding the integrity of the electoral system.

8.   A Government policy discussion paper was published between May 23 - June 10, and over 160 responses were received on the proposals, by the deadline. Discussion meetings were also held with the Association of Electoral Administrators, other returning officers and administrators, suppliers of electoral services and the political parties. On the basis of these comments and responses received during the discussions, the Government recommended a package of additional proposals, primarily focussing on security, to be included in the Act.

These also took into account the recommendations of the Electoral Commission's Securing the vote report, published in May 2005."

A paragraph later they add

"10.   The Act is also part of a wider Government programme of modernising the electoral system, to make it more convenient and accessible, and to pave the way for secure multi-channel voting options. This is necessary for achievement of the Government's target of an "e-enabled general election sometime after 2006".

Much less has been heard on the topic of "e-enabled" General Elections since the last set of e-pilot elections descended into farce (See the chapter on e voting) and there are no more pilots currently planned.

The Act clears up a number of anomalies in existing law – for example, prior to this Act voting age was, of course, eighteen, but the minimum age at which someone could stand for election to Parliament was twenty-one. The Act also makes it possible for an election deposit to be paid by credit or debit card, gives Returning Officers (ROs) a specified period within which to check the validity of nomination papers and to publish the statements of nominated candidates. It gives the Electoral Commission greater powers to specify what constitute election expenses and also, usefully, provides for the Electoral Commission or other bodies (such as the Open Rights Group) to provide official observers at the polls.

However the sections likely to be of most interest to us are those covering registration of electors, anti fraud measures and conduct of elections. The Act creates a criminal offence of applying for a postal or proxy vote "with the intention, in effect, of stealing another person's vote. This can be by a person personating [sic] another elector or by wrongfully redirecting another elector's postal vote." (Explanatory notes to the Electoral Administration Act 2006). It creates a criminal offence of "(c) inducing the registration officer or returning officer to send a postal ballot paper or any communication relating to a postal or proxy vote to an address which has not been agreed to by the person entitled to the vote;

(d) causing a communication relating to a postal or proxy vote or containing a postal ballot paper not to be delivered to the intended recipient " (Electoral Administration Act 2006 S62A)

It also provides powers for the public to object to someone being registered as an elector *after* they have been registered instead of just before as hitherto, a measure so seemingly obvious one can only speculate as to why it wasn't law in the first place. In addition it gives ROs the ability to remove ineligible entries from the register at any time. Both of these are measures it would have been very useful to have in law during the 2005 General Election when journalists and canvassers were wandering through east London finding empty flats with a dozen registered voters. However the cynic might choose to remember the 2000 US Presidential elections when tens of thousands of voters in the swing state of Florida (overwhelmingly, black, Hispanic and registered Democrats) turned up to find that, whether by malice or incompetence they had been purged from the voting rolls as being ineligible to vote whereas in fact they were no such thing.

Unless this power is used very carefully it could easily lead one day to the same angry scenes as in the stolen Birmingham elections where legitimate voters were turned away from polling booths in their hundreds.

Another provision of the Act allows the government to cause what is referred to as a 'keeper' (the Electoral Commision) to set up a Co-ordinated Online Record of Electors, (CORE) gathering together information held by local Electoral Registration Officers (EROs) so that, among other things, duplicate entries could be identified, investigated and where necessary, eliminated. Very helpfully the EAA gives magistrates' courts the power to extend the time limit for criminal prosecutions from twelve months to twenty four upon application by a constable or a Crown Prosecutor. However, an election court, the only means by which an election can actually be overturned rather than a vote rigger prosecuted and a by- election held, is not affected by this and the time limits for calling an election court remain painfully short.

With regard to postal voting the EAA adds certain safeguards to the law. Specifically, anyone applying for a postal or proxy vote will be required to provide the ERO with their personal identifiers – signature and date of birth. The ERO will retain these and match them against the signature and date of birth returned attached to the postal vote itself. If they don't match the vote is invalid.

The Act provides that twenty per cent of postal and proxy votes should be checked but the Association of Electoral Administrators recommends one hundred per cent checking wherever possible.

The Act also provides new rules concerning the safekeeping, inspection and supply or marked registers (that is the register showing which electors have voted, an important security measure) and "provides for the production of marked lists of postal and postal proxy votes" (EAA 2006 explanatory notes).

In addition it alters the time limits for someone to register as an elector on the Electoral Register or to apply for a postal vote from six days before the election to eleven days before the election. (Although the judgement of the Election Court in the case of Simmon v Khan 2007 comments that "this period may itself still be unrealistically short" para 103)

The EAA is obviously encouraging for anyone concerned about vote stealing. It shows that the authorities recognise there is a problem, that that problem focuses around postal votes and it attempts to do something about it. None of the measures are foolish or useless in themselves. Unfortunately they leave gaps that vote riggers can throw a dog through.

Firstly, in Birmingham votes were simply stolen from the post, the voting intention altered and then were sent on. The personal identifiers would have been left unaltered and the votes would have been counted as valid. The new law would have dealt with postal votes being stolen as they went *out* to voters but not as they came back *in.* Ballot thieves may be unscrupulous but that doesn't make them necessarily stupid – they can surely work this out.

Secondly, the discrepancy in personal identifiers ROs are relying on to detect fraud would only occur if the true voter filled in the postal vote application form and the ballot rigger filled in the identifiers attached to the postal vote itself. If I apply for a postal vote on behalf of the unsuspecting Mr Joe Bloggs, fill in the form in my own handwriting, stipulate that the postal ballot itself be sent to an address other than Mr Bloggs' , an address I control (which I can still do, the EAA hasn't altered that at all) and then fill in the postal vote myself no one will be any the wiser unless Mr Bloggs turns up to vote on polling day and is prevented. (The odds of which are about fifty/fifty, much less in most non Parliamentary elections and in many areas of the country.) This happened in many, many cases in Birmingham and elsewhere.

Thirdly, the odds are even better if Mr Bloggs does not exist but is a "ghost voter" invented to pad out the rolls. Ghost voters have always existed but before the Representation of the People Act 2000 with its postal votes on demand someone always had to go into a polling station and impersonate them, a trick that requires a degree of nerve and can only be done a limited number of times to even the dimmest of poll clerks.

Fourthly, as anyone who has ever used a credit card or written a cheque will know, matching signatures is not an exact science which is why most shop workers, in the days before chip and pin, hardly bothered. ROs are hoping to use electronic scanners but these are expensive, temperamental and by no means one hundred per cent reliable either, especially when being operated in the early hours with angry politicians breathing down one's neck.

(It should also be noted that in September 2009 a council by election took place in Birmingham Sparkbrook in which 369 postal ballots were rejected because the signatures did not match up. According to the subsequent police investigation in 359 cases legitimate signatures of the voter had been disallowed – the risks of real votes not being counted is clearly just as great as that of stolen ones making their way in- see the Electoral Commission report on allegations of malpractice in the June 2009 elections, available on the Commission website)

Fifthly, the law stipulates that twenty per cent of postal ballots must be checked. As already mentioned, the Association of Electoral Administrators recommends that one hundred per cent should be checked which is absolutely right from the point of view of the integrity of the election but begs the question of whether this is what will always happen on the ground. As we have seen the more election fraud is going on the more postal and postal proxy votes are likely to be coming in and a smart vote stealer will send them at the last moment, precisely to overwhelm the checkers. In Birmingham, as we have seen, staff were simply overwhelmed, so much so that they failed to follow the laws as they existed then.

This Act creates a major additional set of responsibilities for election staff who have not been guaranteed extra staff, rooms or equipment to deal with them. Those watching them will be politicians or would-be politicians, some or all of whom will be responsible for any vote stealing going on. Indeed Simmons v Khan 2007 goes into this topic in some detail with a clarity I cannot better so I will quote the relevant paragraphs in full

"(112)Clearly, operating the personal identifier system was always going to be very costly in terms of time and resources. If, in theory, the Returning Officer's staff had to compare each PVS [Personal Voting Statement, the signature and D.O.B. returned with the postal vote itself– S.B.] with the appropriate ATV [Application to Vote by post, the signature and D.O.B. sent with the application for a postal vote – S.B.] when the ballot arrives this would greatly add to the labour involved in the process. If, as is likely the bulk of the postal votes arrive at the last minute – they cannot even be sent out to voters until nominations for the election are closed – this will add to the difficulties.

(113) The system also involves a comparison of signatures. Any handwriting expert will tell you – indeed Mr Hughes the handwriting expert called to give evidence did tell me – that one of the most difficult tasks that a handwriting expert can be called on to perform is the comparison of two signatures, one genuine and the other suspect, with no other material to help in the task. It requires great expertise to distinguish between a deliberate forgery and a genuine signature which comes within the range of variation that we all produce in our signatures. In many cases even the most skilled handwriting expert has to confess himself unable to give a reliable opinion.

(114) Those most at risk of having a genuine signature mistaken for a forgery are, of course, also the most vulnerable, such as the elderly, the poorly literate and those for whom neither English nor Roman script are matters of everyday familiarity.

(115) Nonetheless signature comparison is the task that is imposed on the Returning Officer's staff, officials who have no training in handwriting identification and are working under increasing pressure as the election approaches.

(116)It may be safely said, however, that there is no problem so bad that the enthusiastic application of electronic technology cannot make it a good deal worse. Election authorities at both national and local level have been encouraged to use computer programmes designed to perform the signature comparison. Comparison of signatures by computer is inevitably even more haphazard than comparison by untrained staff using eyes and brain. The experience of the electronic system has therefore been that the computer rejects very large numbers of entirely genuine signatures leaving the Returning Officer with the unenviable choice between

(a)   getting his staff to check the rejected documents manually; or

(b)   accepting the computer's verdict with the risk of disenfranchising a large number of honest postal voters "

The pressure to get a swift election result will be as heavy as ever. Under the circumstances it is very easy to see harassed staff (who by the *start* of the count may have been going for sixteen or seventeen hours solid) eliminating those fake votes they find in the mandatory twenty per cent checked but not sorting through the remaining eighty per cent in search of others. If the election then turns into a knife edge finish the pressure to keep quiet would be huge.

Election staff are only human and for those not hired for the day elections are usually a very small part of what they do – they have other roles and responsibilities to get on with in their council work and want the minimum of friction and controversy with councillors who are either the ones being voted for or (in the case of Parliamentary and Euro elections) their political friends and allies.

Lastly of course, and most importantly, even if not one of the above applies *the postal vote is not a secret ballot.* Thugs can threaten people. Family members – husbands, wives, parents, can put pressure on. Canvassers, elders, priests, people pretending to be officials, bosses, councillors, anyone with a position of authority or a glib tongue can call and take away postal ballots that have been signed but the vote not cast – or ballots where it has, and alter the vote. People can be bribed. These are the most insidious form of vote stealing of all because they are invisible – the victims will almost never come forward.

The next chapter will cover a well known case of ballot rigging since the Electoral Administration Act of 2006 – and one which that Act failed utterly to stop.

A Spectre Is Haunting Slough – Ghost Voters and Election Rigging

In Birmingham, as we have seen, much of the vote stealing going on was exactly that – the stealing of votes from people who really did exist and were legitimately on the electoral register. In the 2007 local elections in Slough a rather different method was used – the deliberate 'padding' of the electoral roll with what are sometimes called ghost voters.

This case is also significant in that it was the first case to be heard by an election court following the passing of the Electoral Administration Act of 2006. It thus offered an opportunity to see if that act was succeeding in its stated aim of creating the "lowest possible fraud" (www.opsi.gov.uk/acts/acts2006)

As with the Birmingham case we have the advantage that the whole criminal conspiracy was exposed in court and those responsible convicted – we do not have to fear libel law and the information is available in the public domain. The whole of the judgement can be found online at www.slough.info/law/law41/law41.html .

As at Birmingham the case was heard by Election Commissioner Mr Richard Mawrey QC (NB the election commissioner is the one appointed to hear a case in an election court and should in no way be confused with the Electoral Commission, an official government body) who was able to draw comparisons with the Birmingham case.

Unlike Birmingham the election court only heard a challenge to the election in one ward, the Central Borough ward in Slough for the election held on the 3rd of May. In this ward local Conservative businessman Eshaq Khan had seemingly beaten his Labour opponent Lydia Simmons by one hundred and twenty votes in a striking defiance of local trends. However around four hundred and fifty voters had been added to the electoral rolls in the run up to the election. Labour cried "foul" and took the political and financial risk of bringing an election petition.   The case rested on proving the belief of the Labour Party and its candidate, Ms Simmons that some or all of these voters were not legitimately on the electoral register, either because they were not eligible to vote or did not exist. This belief turned out to be absolutely correct. Mr Mawrey had this to say on the topic of this method of vote rigging.

"Those masters of the pithy phrase, the Australians, call it "roll-stuffing" – the "roll" being, of course, the Electoral Roll or Register.

(124) What roll stuffing involves is casting votes by using names which appear on the Electoral Register but which relate to people who have no right to be on the Register...

(126) How does it come about that roll stuffing is so easy in Great Britain?

(127) The system of registering voters in Great Britain maybe fairly described as shambolic. ...

(128) The British system is not adopted by any of our neighbours

129)In essence voter registration in Great Britain is a system for putting names on to the Register. Provided names get on the Register, it appears to be a matter of complete indifference as to how they get there, and the system contains no mechanism whatsoever for verifying that the names on the Register are properly included - or indeed that the names relate to real people. In a period when the citizen is required to produce his passport and a
utilities bill even to open a very small bank account, registration for the highest duty of the
citizen, that of choosing his government, requires no verification at all.

(130) Each ERO is obliged by s 10 of the 1983 Act to conduct an annual canvass with reference to the date of 15th October in each year. This is a household canvass, meaning that each unit which is or appears to be a separate dwelling is sent a registration form.

(131) In the past, the form used to be a blank registration form inviting the head of the household

to fill in the names of all those resident in the dwelling on 15th October in that year who were (or would become in the next year) of sufficient age to vote and were otherwise eligible to vote. The form had to be signed by a member of the household.

(132) In order to streamline the process, however, the habit of most ERO is to send out the form pre-printed with the names of those who were registered for that household for the previous year, inviting the recipient to confirm, delete or add names on the list. In many areas the recipient is invited to use the internet to respond and is provided with a PIN, printed on the form, to facilitate this. In most cases the recipient is requested to use the internet only if the existing details are to be confirmed and to return the paper form itself if there are any changes. Some authorities even permit amendment of the form online. There is - there can be - no independent verification of the stated identity of the person sending the information to the ERO whether on paper or by internet.

(133) What happens if the form is not returned ? No figures for the national average were produced to the court but Mr Quayle told me that the level of return in Slough was about 73%. Where the remaining forms are concerned, many authorities will try to fill the gap by making house to house enquiries but there will always be a considerable number of properties where there is no return.

(134) Common sense might dictate that if a household did not return the form the existing names should be removed from the Register, leaving any inhabitants to re-apply if they felt strongly enough. Such, however, is the fear that one voter might, by inertia, be lost from the Register that the

almost universal habit is to keep the names on the Register for at least one more year.

(135) It would be hard to devise a worse system of voter registration. Even if the system is working entirely honestly, there will inevitably be a large number of names on the Register of people who no longer have the right to vote because they no longer occupy the property against which they are registered. For example, Mr A registers himself in the annual canvass as resident at 1 Station Road on 15th October 2004. In December 2004 he moves to the other end of the country. In October 2005, the occupants of 1 Station Road do not bother to return the form or return it with Mr A's name still on it. At any time up to (at the earliest) October 2006, Mr A's name will remain on the Register and a vote cast in that name will be accepted by the Returning Officer.

(136) In any community this system provides a fraudster's paradise. In areas with a mobile and transient population, the temptation to fraud must be almost irresistible. Imagine a property which is always in multiple occupation with, say, fifteen people living there. The occupants never stay long and are constantly being replaced. The owner of the property receives the household registration form with fifteen names on it. He knows that they have all left but, by simply signing the form unaltered or by confirming it online or even by doing nothing, those fifteen names will remain on the Register and will provide fifteen votes that can safely be used by him for whichever candidate takes his fancy.

(137) The Electoral Register is, of course, a public document. Anybody may obtain a copy. The unscrupulous local political activist can thus obtain his own copy, carry out a few discreet enquiries, discover that a considerable number of the names on the Register relate to people who no longer live at the address shown and take steps to appropriate their votes accordingly.

(138) But the Register is not writ in stone on 15th October. It is a "live" Register. Any eligible person moving into the area may apply to put himself on the Register at any time. The only slight impediment is that mentioned above, namely that application to be placed on the Register must be made not less than eleven days before an election if the applicant wishes to vote at that election.

(139) Application is simplicity itself. A form (the AFR) is filled in and sent to the ERO. This requires no information beyond the name and address of the elector. Amazingly, the applicant is not even obliged to provide his personal identifier. The registration of the elector is purely mechanical. Provided the form seems to be in order, the ERO must add the name to the Register. No form of verification is required: no enquiries are or can be made: the name is added. Even though the application may be and usually is signed, there is no mechanism for comparing the signatures on the AFR with the signatures on any ATV (postal vote application) or on the PVS which accompanies the ballot paper.

(140) Nothing therefore could be easier than to register false names on the Register for the purposes of exercising their votes. **What is the point of such a registration system?**

(141) It may be asked what possible point there could be in a registration system such as that currently in force which, even if operated honestly, results in huge numbers of "dead names" remaining on the Register. Those dead names obviously inflate the apparent size of the electorate but, absent fraud, equally obviously they cannot vote.

(142) The inflated Register clearly involves additional work for the ERO but, more importantly, the Register provides the basis, indeed the only basis, for calculating the size of the electorate at any given election.

(143) The irony is this. What prompted the whole disastrous experiment of postal voting on demand in the first place was the perception of

politicians that voter turnout percentages were too low. But the recorded percentages themselves were inevitably being falsified by the dead names on the Register. If the apparent electorate is inflated by dead names, the actual votes cast must mathematically be a smaller percentage than would be the case if the "total electorate" against which they are compared were to be confined to those actually entitled to vote.

(144) Assume an electoral area has 100 votes on the Register. 20 of them are dead names. 60 votes are cast at the election. Under present methods of calculation those 60 votes are expressed as a percentage of the nominal electorate - 60/100 and thus 60%. Low turnout – general gloom. The real calculation is, of course: persons actually entitled to vote 80: votes cast 60: percentage turnout 60/80 and thus 75%. High turnout - general rejoicing.

(145) It may be asked, therefore, why should one maintain an electoral registration system different from that of our democratic neighbours, which delivers artificially deflated voter turnout percentages leading to the introduction of ill-considered changes to the electoral process in the hope of increasing turnout?

Registration and postal voting

(146) Before the introduction of postal voting on demand, the problem of roll-stuffing was containable. Where votes had to be cast in person, anyone wanting to use false names on the Register to cast votes had to produce actual voters who were prepared to go to polling stations to cast the votes. If the false name being used was that of a person who had once lived at the property but had moved on or died, there was always the risk that someone at the polling station might have known the real voter whose name was being used and who would thus unmask the imposter.

(147) The sheer logistics of this species of personation thus made it impracticable to record more than a relatively small number of bogus votes. If the constituency or ward had a small population and the contest was likely to be very close, this kind of tactic might just be sufficiently viable to justify the risks involved.

(148) Postal voting on demand swept away all these worries for the fraudster. Gone was the risk that the bogus voter might be recognised at the poll. False names on the Register could be used wholesale to cast bogus votes in their hundreds with only minuscule risk of detection.

(149) And the personal identifiers, paradoxically, made it easier. If a fraudster registers a fictitious person on the Register and applies for a postal vote, he can easily ensure that the ATV and the subsequent PVS of that fictitious person contain the same signature and date of birth. All he need do is keep a photocopy of the ATV to remind him when he comes to fill in the PVS. From the Returning Officer's point of view the vote is perfectly regular - the personal identifiers match exactly. They are, however, the personal identifiers of a non-existent person.

(150) Mr Millar referred to these false names on the Register as "ghost voters", a useful term, though the votes they cast were far from phantasmal.

(151) Postal voting on demand, therefore, put the roll-stuffers in business in a big way. "(Simmon v Khan)

One interesting feature of the trial is that the Conservatives, that is those who were effectively the defendants, had the previous year repeatedly alleged to Mr Quayle, who is both the Returning Officer and the Electoral Registration Officer in Slough that their Labour opponents were roll-stuffing, in particular by registering to vote in more than one ward. They went out of their way to make this clear to the court. That said, they did not bring an election petition to challenge the 2006 election. In the light of this it may well be that these allegations were deliberate and slanderous attempts to muddy the waters in the eyes of the court and the public and darken the reputations of their blameless opponents.

On the other hand, given the expenses and difficulties involved in an election petition, as laid out in the chapter on the Birmingham vote rigging, *not* bringing one mighthave been a perfectly rational decision, even if the Conservatives believed their own claims. If they did (regardless of how unfounded that belief and those claims were) it might go some way to explain their actions in 2007.

For reasons which are obvious, canvassers of all parties were out and about in Central Borough ward in the run up to the local elections trying to identify their supporters so that they could get them out on polling day. This was given particular urgency by the large number of voters (449) who had registered in the six weeks before polling day, almost invariably voters with Asian names. There is nothing remotely unusual about voters with Asian names in Slough, it is home to some of the UK's proportionately largest populations of Asian origin. What was unusual was the sudden influx. Slough's Asian communities are long established and most recent immigrants have been from Eastern Europe. The next highest number of new registrations in Slough were the 286 in Chalvey ward, which were themselves far higher than the average and led to further suspicions in their own right. A Mr Safdar Ali, Chair of the Slough Constituency Labour Party was disturbed to see names which he thought he recognised as belonging to genuine voters – but who lived in other parts of the town. Canvassers in Central Borough were sent out to investigate and began to smell the proverbial rat the day they canvassed Hawtrey Close.

No fewer than nineteen voters, all with the aforementioned Asian names had registered in the last week before registrations closed. Six were at No. 4, another six at No. 6 and seven at Nos 8-10 Hawtrey Close.

However, No. 4 turned out to be inhabited by a Polish couple who were quite adamant that they weren't hiding any voters on the premises, Asian or otherwise. No. 6 was a derelict and boarded up house and Nos 8-10 an equally derelict and more importantly, equally empty, former old people's home.

Every single one of the nineteen non-existent voters of Hawtrey Close had applied for, and been sent a postal vote. Furthermore

"This was perhaps the most dramatic finding of the team but enquiries at other properties revealed that considerable numbers of newly registered voters were not living in the houses where they had been registered. Clearly roll-stuffing had been taking place." (Simmons v Khan)

Naturally Labour's team drew this to the attention of Mr Quayle and equally naturally there was nothing he could do to strike those voters off the register at such short notice. At the election Mr Eshaq Khan was declared the winner with 1439 votes to Ms Simmons' 1319.

The procedure to remove a voter from the electoral register requires the Electoral Registration Officer to write to them at the address rovided in order that legitimate voters may have the opportunity to submit evidence and/or attend a hearing to demonstrate that they are legitimate.

Without this safeguard life for vote stealers would beeven easier – they could simply have anyone they don't know to be one of their supporters removed from the electoral register a few days before the election and winhands down – always assuming their opponents hadn't done the same thing first.

There was no chance of completing the process in Slough before the election. These facts are of course well known to those who add phantom voters to the register which is why they tend to do so at the last minute. Even if bogus voters were removed from the register *after* the election their votes would still be treated as having *been* valid for the period of the election itself – in order to overturn Mr Eshaq's fraudulent victory the expense and risks of an election petition still remained the only option for the "defeated" candidate, Ms Lydia Simmons. This petition was duly presented on 24th May 2007, the last possible date that this could have been done.

Mawrey describes the election petition as both "ambiguous" and "exiguous", not surprisingly given that evidence was being gathered in a relatively short period of time by people with no legal training or police powers. (Simmons v Khan para 199) It was, however, adequate for the case to go ahead. In his judgement Mawrey reviews the options available to Mr Eshaq Khan, chosen candidate of Slough's army of ghosts.

"The choices facing him were, essentially, twofold. First he could play safe and adopt a strategy of denying any participation in electoral fraud by himself or his agents. With a modicum of good fortune for Mr Eshaq Khan, Ms Simmons might fail to establish wrongdoing by Mr Eshaq Khan or his agents [this refers not simply to Mr Khan's designated election agent but to anyone acting on his behalf – S.B.] – particularly as this would have to be proved to the criminal standard of proof – and she might thus be thrown back on a case based on general corruption under s 164 of the 1983 Act. Although proving general corruption itself might not be an insuperable obstacle, Ms Simmons might well fail to establish it to a sufficient degree as to make it likely that the corruption affected the result of the election, particularly as Mr Eshaq Khan's winning majority was a respectable 120 votes. If Ms Simmons failed to prove a likely effect on the result, the Petition would fail." (Simmons v Khan para 209)

If this had happened of course, Ms Simmons and her party would have been faced not only with their own legal bills but very possibly with Mr Khan's costs as well. The weaknesses of our election petition system, where corruption can be proved but the result stand and objectors be penalised because they cannot *prove* the result was changed would have struck again, acting as a terrible object lesson *not* to challenge vote rigging.

Fortunately for Ms Simmons, the Slough Labour Party and the rest of us Mr Khan decided to go for thehigh risk option of denying that there had been any significant false registration at all.

Part of the evidence consisted of the records of Labour's challenges to names on the electoral register following the election. Getting these voters struck from the rolls, as we have seen, could not possibly overturn the election result but the more voters on the roll who should not have been that the petitioners could show, the stronger their initial case. A full case of course, could not be built without showing who these bogus voters had voted for. (Other election petitions have been dropped because suspected stolen or ghost votes have been cast for several different candidates, ironically, because this is far better evidence of general corruption in the broadest sense than if they had all been cast for one. In the immortal words of 'Carry On' "They're all at it!")

Also the petitioners had simply not had the time and people available to challenge every one of the possible ghost voters. They had focussed on what they considered the most blatant cases and eventually made a total of two hundred and nine challenges.

Of these Mr Quayle, the ERO agreed to remove one hundred and forty five from the register. This is already a high percentage and Mawrey commented"..the fact that the remaining 64 were retained on the

Register is no guarantee of their being genuinely on theRegister. Mr Quayle very properly worked on the basis of giving those who resisted the challenges the benefit of the doubt wherever possible and, in the initial stages, Mr Quayle undoubtedly (and properly) accepted as genuine documents which subsequent investigation have shown to be spurious." (Simmons v Khan para 217)

Ms Simmons and her supporters were able to match up this list of voters purged with the list of postal votes cast and show that one hundred and twelve were cast for Mr Khan (and three rejected because the relevant signatures did not match), these votes all purportedly coming from a mere thirty-one properties.

However, Mr Eshaq Khan and his team had apparently already decided upon a strategy of "proving" that a substantial number of the "ghost" voters were real and entitled to vote. It was to be a fateful decision.

Many of the sixty-four voters challenged by Simmons &Co. who Mr Quayle had left on the register had been left there because he had been provided with tenancy agreements in their names.

"Bright ideas, alas can be carried too far." was Mawrey's mordant comment (Simmons v Khan para 223)

"The drawback was that these tenancy agreements were, to all intents and purposes, identical. They had quite obviously been produced from a single computer-generated template file and filled in with (some) of the relevant details. All were incomplete in certain respects (the same respects) and most displayed a strange inability to produce a consistent typeface for the details entered into the template. Most of the documents did not, on examination, even purport to show a tenancy granted by the owner of the property. Most showed what would be, if the document itself were genuine, an attempt by an existing tenant to grant a sub-tenancy which that tenant had no power to grant." (Simmons v Khan para 224)

This last of course would not in itself be significant for the purposes of an election court - being an unauthorised sub-tenant does not deprive someone of their right to vote, although, interestingly it *would* enable massive pressure to be put on them by the landlord or main tenant to hand over their postal ballot. However with the other discrepancies it does help provide strong evidence that these "tenancy agreements" had been created purely for the purpose of providing false evidence.

After the first few Mr Quayle ceased to accept these as evidence. Mr Mawrey concluded "the evidence before me left me in no doubt that the ten tenancy agreements ...were forgeries, deliberately concocted for the purposes of deceiving Mr Quayle into rejecting the Labour challenges to the Register.

These forgeries were not random pieces of dishonesty by unconnected individuals. They were, on their face, the product of a concerted campaign to resist the challenges to the Register. Given the identities of those who were concerting the campaign to resist the challenge, the inferences capable of being drawn by the court as to the respective merits of the parties to the Petition do not need to be spelled out." (Simmons v Khan paras 227-228)

Nevertheless Mr Eshaq and his solicitors made determined efforts in court in the teeth of an impressive array of evidence against them. When the owner of the relevant buildings in Hawtrey Close, local businessman Mohammed Azam testified that two were indeed boarded up and the third inhabited by a Polish family, Mr Price, the Conservative's lawyer produced a statement from the landlord's rent collector to the effect that he had had problems with both break ins and squatters during 2006 and 2007 and proceeded to cross examine with gusto. As Mawrey says Mr Price " wisely stopped short of taxing the court's credulity by suggesting that nineteen Asians had broken into the properties for the purposes of registering as voters and exercising postal votes for Mr Eshaq Khan and had then silently stolen away." (Simmons v Khan para 252) but this was clearly the implication.

The next street to be the topic of evidence was Richmond Crescent where there were six voters of Asian names registered at No. 43 and seven at No. 41. Ms Simmons task was enviably simple. She simply called as witnesses Edyta Jankowska and Skora Bozena, two Polish ladies who actually lived at No. 43 and No. 41 respectively. The only possible option for the vote riggers and their solicitors was to give up on the ghost voters registered at these addresses altogether and hope for better luck on the others (an increasingly forlorn hope as proceedings went on) or to call the witnesses liars.

The lawyer, Mr Price whose task Mawrey rightly called unenviable "..at the end of the day... could not bring himself to suggest to Ms Jankowska that she was lying. In this he was absolutely right and his decision is what one would have expected from the consummate professionalism with which he conducted Mr Eshaq Khan's case." (Simmons v Khan para 258)

Ms Skora Bozena was also quite clear that there were no Asian postal voters lurking in her home but significantly she did explain that "..mail did arrive for people with non-Polish names which was collected by the man who collects the rent for her landlord, a Mr Khan. In April 2007 a lot of brown envelopes arrived for the non-resident names and when the rent-collector took them away he said they were election letters." (Simmons v Khan para 259)

Whether out of desperation or sheer chutzpah Mr Eshaq Khan decided to call as witness a Mr Mahboob Khan, one of his election team, who testified that the thirteen disputed voters were indeed living at 41 and 43 and the witnesses were lying. When asked to suggested a reason why they would he responded with what Mawrey rightly calls " a deplorable piece of racism, suggesting that it was well known that Poles were "easily manipulated" and would, in effect, do anything for the promise of a job or a house." (Simmons v Khan para 261) He did himself no favours at all with Mawrey whose judgement describes his evidence as "a pack of lies from start to finish." (Simmons v Khan para 262)

17 Diamond Road where eight non existent voters were registered, seven of whom voted for Eshaq Khan and one of whom had their vote disallowed passed without any real attempt to pretend the "voters" were real. Not so 13 Princes Street where Mr Khan's team had given Mr Quayle, the ERO a statement, purportedly from Mr Mohammed Raza, who no one disputes has lived at the address with his wife Mrs Aziza Raza and their three children since June 2006. This statement, backed up yet again by a bogus tenancy agreement, gives a detailed account of how the four disputed individuals moved into the Raza's home in December 2006 and then moved out in June 2007 shortly after casting their postal votes for Mr Eshaq Khan in the elections.

Mrs Raza appeared as a witness in the court and unhesitatingly explained that she had no knowledge of the four who had supposedly shared her home for months, that both the statement and the tenancy agreement produced by Mr Khan's team were forgeries and that the signatures on them were not her husband's. "What she proved, therefore, was not simply that the four ghost voters had not been residing at 13 Princes Street but that Mr Eshaq Khan's team had resorted to forgery in their attempt to persuade Mr Quayle to keep these four names on the Register." (Simmons v Khan para 268)

In the next, 47 Diamond Road , a determined attempt was made to "nobble" the witness. Mrs Nighat Khan had provided a witness statement testifying that the five disputed voters registered at her property did not, and never had, lived there but on day three of the election court a typed letter arrived signed by Mrs Khan withdrawing her statement and claiming that she was too ill to attend the court. The court was having none of it and issued a witness summons.

In court Mrs Khan explained that she had not been ill nor did she wish to change what she had said in her statement but had been very ervous about appearing in court. A gentleman, speaking good Urdu and claiming to be a lawyer had come to see her with the letter already typed and had persuaded her that if she only signed it she could escape the whole ordeal.

The identity of the persuasive Urdu speaker was never established – one thing that can be said for certain is that it was definitely not anyone connected with the lawyers retained by the vote riggers. Indeed Mawrey goes out of his way to praise their integrity and professionalism. None of the statements or documents which proved to be forgeries or lies had been taken or produced by them but by Mr Khan or his friends and supporters. Whatever else can be said against Mr Khan he seems to have secured the services of some excellent lawyers and it is no fault of theirs that they were faced with a difficult case and some deeply implausible witnesses.

It was shortly after this that perhaps the most implausible of all those witnesses hove into view, Mr Mohammed Basharat Khan. 3 Charlotte Avenue is a two bedroomed flat inhabited by a married couple, Mrs Perveen, Mr Zahid and their five children. According to the impressively sanguine Mr Khan apparently all seven were either deeply unobservant, very forgetful or above such mundane matters as concern over living space.

The reason I say this is because the case for the defence depended entirely on the claim that six adults had moved into this already somewhat crowded apartment in April 2007 – just in time to register to vote – and moved out again shortly after the elections.

Mrs Perveen had already testified that none of the six had ever lived at her home. Undeterred, Mohammed Khan took the witness box to explain why she was mistaken.

"What he said was that his brother Gulzeb Khan, Gulzeb's wife, Naseen Khan, daughters Iram Gul Khan and Uzma Khan, son Habib Khan and nephew Adeel Abbas had been living at an address in Walthamstow in east London. In April 2007, however, the whim came to them that Slough was the place to live. So they decamped, bag and baggage, to Slough where, on the strength of some (unspecified) family relationship they contacted Ms Perveen and her husband...[who] were, of course, only too delighted to accommodate Gulzeb Khan and his extended family and they came to an arrangement whereby the Walthamstow Six moved into the two-bedroomed flat at 3 Charlotte Close. Ms Perveen, her husband and their five children, he claimed, obligingly agreed that they would all go to her father's house to sleep at nights but otherwise the family continued to occupy the flat." (Simmons v Khan para 277)

The judge seems to have been reluctantly impressed by the sheer brass neck of all this. "One did not know which to admire more – the insouciance with which this absurd cock-and-bull story was narrated to the court or the contempt for the court's intelligence in supposing for an instant that any court would fall for it." (Simmons v Khan para 280) The court concluded that the Walthamstow Six had never left Walthamstow.

Nor was this the end of the resourceful Mr Mohammed Khan's involvement. He himself, at the time of the election, had been registered in two wards, Central Borough and the neighbouring Wexham Lea. His explanation was that his home in Wexham Lea, 57 Mirador Crescent had been uninhabitable because of renovations so he had moved into

Central Borough, where he, his wife and his sister-in-law had all cast postal votes for Mr Eshaq Khan.

For some reason, possibly connected with the fact that he had clearly not received post addressed to the Central Borough residence at the time and thus had needed to obtain duplicate postal voting packages from the Town Hall, or possibly connected to the fact that the Wexham Lea address was apparently inhabited by four adults at the time it was supposed to be empty, the court did not believe him.

This gentleman turned out to be one of a considerable number who were registered in both Central Borough and Wexham Lea and who apparently moved back to Wexham Lea almost immediately after the election. It should be noted that while they seem to have had no legitimate right to vote in the Central Borough ward they were at least not voting twice as there was no Conservative candidate in Wexham Lea that year.

Nor was Wexham Lea the only area from which voters were travelling to show their loyalty to the Conservative cause. In Richmond Crescent, described in the judgement as "richer in ghosts than the Tower of London" (Simmons v Khan para 291) with thirty-eight non-existent voters in ten properties a Mr Gulnawaz Khan had four relatives move over from Kashmir, moving into his son's room for the period of the election while said son was on holiday. How these relatives came to be eligible to vote in a British election was not explained, indeed clearly *could not* be explained – except with reference to the flaws in the UK's system of voter registration referred to earlier. The court was unimpressed.

The court had also been faced with a file consisting of forty-six witness statements obtained by Mr Eshaq Khan and his supporters. (Again, *not* by Mr Khan's solicitors)

"The overwhelming majority of these statements were, in my judgement, entirely fraudulent. Even if they were made by the people in whose names they appear, those people were induced by Mr Eshaq Khan and his team to make those statements with, in each case, both the person making the statement and the person taking the statement being well aware that its contents were untrue." (Simmons v Khan para 305)

The final phase of evidence concerned the handwriting on the personal voter statements and the applications for postal votes. This section of the court's conclusions rests largely upon the evidence of a Mr Hughes, a handwriting expert retained by Ms Simmons, whose evidence, however, was broadly accepted by Mr Eshaq Khan's team.

The handwriting was largely that of five people, each of them having filled in a considerable number of documents. There is nothing illegal about this – provided the signature is, or appears to be that of the voter anyone can fill in the forms.

"Whether it is sensible to permit this is another matter and one on which the court (and the Council of Europe) may take a different view from that of Parliament, but that is the legal position. "If it can be shown, however, that the hand completing the documents has completed a considerable number of forms which can be demonstrated to be fraudulent, that is another matter entirely. And that is what happened in Slough." (Simmons v Khan paras 312-3)

The largest number of forms, one hundred and ninety-eight, had been filled in by Mr Mohammed Basharat Khan,the gentleman whose extended family had moved into Slough for the period of the elections without ever being noticed by the other seven inhabitants of the two bedroomed apartment. The next largest group, seventy-nine, were completed by the candidate, Mr Eshaq Khan himself.

In both cases the court concluded that those completing the forms had been involved in the false registration of voters. The three authors of the other groupings were not identified but as the court concluded "It would be perverse to suppose however, that they were not members of Mr Eshaq Khan's team." (Simmons v Khan para 322)

There were also twenty-five cases where the relevant signatures did not match (all of them being postal votes cast for Mr Eshaq Khan). Evidently the forgeries were well done – it had taken a handwriting expert to spot them. There is every reason to think that there may have been others that were not among the examples presented to Mr Hughes for examination – as has been said earlier, the examples were exactly that and almost certainly did not cover every ghost voter.

As hardly needs to be said, not only did Mr Khan have his victory overturned, the court describing him and his witnesses as "a pitifully inept bunch of liars" (Simmons vKhan para 330) but he and several of his witnesses were arrested and tried for a variety of criminal offences. In May 2009 Mr Eshaq Khan, Mr Mahboob Khan, Mr Mohammed Basharat Khan, Mr Altaf Khan, Mr Gulnawaz Khan and Mr Arshad Raja received sentences ranging from four and a half years to eight months. Charles Miskin, prosecuting for the Crown said "Postal voting has been in high demand and as a result there has been a surge of ballot fixing, the like of which has not been seen since Victorian times." (Mail 02/05/2009)

Reporting on the case John Morrison in the Guardian wrote "All parties are so desperate to reverse a slump in electoral turnout that they have connived with each other to do anything to make voting easier, but it's clear that the government has led the way using the equivalent of monosodium glutamate in the electoral kitchen...In my view...the government knows perfectly well what is going on and takes the view that a little bit of electoral fraud doesn't really matter, because Labour stands to gain most from higher turnouts." (Guardian 21/03/2008) He also pointed out that the Electoral Commision report "Securing the vote" (to which the Electoral Administration Act of 2006 had supposedly been a response) had admitted that only when votes were cast in a polling booth could they be guaranteed to be free from improper influence.

Some may consider this too harsh an assessment – after all the vote riggers were caught and were punished. However Election Commisioner Mawrey concluded that it very nearly wasn't so. "I have been appalled by the ease with which these substantial frauds were committed. The only reasons they came to light at all were the incompetence of the fraudsters and the blatant nature of the frauds. If Mr Eshaq Khan and his team had been able to resist the temptation of Hawtrey Close and, to a lesser extent , 3 Charlotte Avenue and the Polish ladies of Richmond Crescent, Mr Eshaq Khan might well have been safe in his council seat.

There is no reason to suppose that this is an isolated incident. Roll stuffing is childishly simple to commit and *very difficult to detect. To ignore the possibility that it is widespread, especially in local elections, is a policy that even an ostrich would despise."* [Emphasis added S.B.] (Simmons v Khan paras 345-6)

The implications are obvious: more careful vote riggers could and probably *have* succeeded without their activities being brought to light. Nor is there any reason to think that Parliamentary elections are less vulnerable – indeed with the greater number of voters over a wider area it would be harder, if anything, to produce enough proven examples of stolen votes to prove that the result of the election had been altered.

As Mawrey also points out, the postal voting system wasintroduced on the back of the belief that falling turnout was a by-product of the alleged difficulty of voting. "One can well see that, for professional politicians, the alternative rationale, namely that voters are disillusioned with politics and politicians and indifferent to their activities, is unthinkable." (Simmons v Khan para 347)

Nevertheless, in say, the French Presidential elections of 2007, with their twelve candidates covering the whole of the political spectrum the turnout reached eighty-five per cent before falling back to a mere sixty per cent for the National Assembly elections. This, together with the fact that registration is more difficult in France and there is no such thing as a postal vote, suggests that voters will turn out when there is an alternative they would actually like to vote for.

Elsewhere in his judgement Commissioner Mawrey points out that there were fourteen different types of fraud identified in the Birmingham elections and the Electoral Administration Act would only have blocked one of them. Slough's army of ghosts he described as "The Fifteenth Fraud". The EAA 2006 wouldn't have stopped that either.

The judgement in the case of Simmons v Khan ends with the words

"I concluded the Birmingham judgement with the words *The systems to deal with fraud are not working well. They are not working badly. The fact is that there are no systems to deal realistically with fraud and there never have been. Until there are fraud will continue unabated.* It would have been pleasant to conclude this judgement by saying that this had now all changed. But I cannot. Despite the 2006 Act the opportunities for easy and effective electoral fraud remain substantially as they were on 4th April 2005." (Simmons v Khan paras 351-2)

Reporting the case for the Times Dominic Kennedy, who had helped expose widespread vote rigging in the North of England at the 2004 elections stated   "The Conservatives have exploited the new rules eagerly, using technology to trick voters into sending their ballots to Tory-controlled addresses. The seats with most postal votes in the last general election showed bigger swings to the Conservatives. This conspiracy goes a lot wider than Birmingham, Slough or Labour." (Times 19/03/2008)

The government's anti-fraud measures had proved completely ineffective. Britain still remained the best place in Western Europe to try to rig an election and a country where the secret ballot was under threat. It is hard to imagine such laxness being tolerated in any other kind of ballot. Indeed in December 2009 a British court granted an injunction preventing BA staff from striking because of minor irregularities in the ballot, in that a small number of union members had been balloted who would not still be working for British Airways at the time of the strike. This is despite the fact that the union had no way of knowing these members had decided to leave their employment (the employer refused to share information with them) and despite the fact that all parties agreed the result of the ballot would not have been changed and it had been carried out in good faith throughout. (The Socialist 17/12/2009). As we have seen, the state of the UK Electoral Register means that if governments and local authorities were held to the same standard as trades unions it is unlikely that any election would ever be declared valid. This is also despite the fact that unions have no powers to force their membership to strike even when not doing so is a clear defiance of a democratic ballot. Since the passing of the Civil Contingencies Act of 2004 the British government has almost unlimited powers in the event of a state of emergency – and complete leeway to decide what constitutes a state of emergency. ("Whose Side Are They On?" Alan Pearce)

Nor was it only journalists and judges whose business it was to know about these things that were starting to take notice of the increasing possibilities for fraud in British elections– no fewer than three official reports were being issued over the years 2007-8. It is to these that we shall now turn.

The Whole World Is Watching

On 28th June 2006 a number of parliamentarians from several different parties and countries led by a Conservative MP from the UK, Mr James Wilshire, put forward a motion to request the Council of Europe to begin a monitoring procedure to ensure that the UK was meeting its obligations under the European Convention on Human Rights.

The specific obligation the signatories had in mind was the obligation under Article 3 of the Convention of "The High Contracting Parties" that is to say the governments of the EU "to hold free elections...which will ensure the free expression of the opinion of the people in the choice of the legislature". The contention of those signing the motion was that there was enough fraud involved in the system of postal voting on demand that the UK was failing to do this.

It should be noted that it is not easy to meet the conditions for putting forward a motion of this kind. If it was signed mainly or solely by the opposition parties of the country concerned we might be able to fairly regard itas a piece of political manouevring. In fact it requires parliamentarians from at least five different countries and two political groups.

(Most MEPs whatever their domestic allegiances are grouped in cross-border organisations such as the European People's Party which represents most moderate Conservative groups. Fascists have had difficulty maintaining cross border alliances not least because the Italian neo-fascists accused all Romanians of being thieves, the Hungarian fascists want to annex part of Romania, the Romanian fascists want to expel all ethnic Hungarians and many of the West European fascists have issues with East Europeans.)

It is true that the signatories are predominantly Conservatives and their European allies – however this does not mean their case should be dismissed out of hand. UK Labour MPs such as Ann Cryer and Marsha Singh have willingly used Parliament to air their convictions (backed up by actual court convictions of politicians in Mr Singh's city of Bradford) that vote stealing has gone on.

A Labour MEP might hesitate to sign, not only because of party loyalty but because MEPs in Britain are elected by what is called the "closed list " system. What this means is that voters are unable to vote for an individual candidate but have to vote for a "slate", a list of candidates pre-selected by a party. The higher up that list the candidates name is placed the better his or her chances of election – and it is the party machine, not the voters who decide the placings on the list.

The careers of a number of well known left wing MEPs came to an abrupt end when this system was introduced, most notably Hugh Kerr and Ken Coates, Chair of the Bertrand Russell Peace Foundation who criticised the closed list system as undemocratic and likely to stifle dissent. They were then expelled by Labour functionaries apparently blissfully unaware that they were proving the point.

The parliamentarians' application emphasised the Mawrey judgement in Birmingham and the fact that subsequent to that a senior staff member at Birmingham council was suspended when a thousand postal ballots were found in the office that had clearly not been counted.

Furthermore they pointed out that at the time the motion was brought there were investigations going on into possible vote rigging in Birmingham (again), Coventry, Woking and no fewer than seven London boroughs in relation to the local elections of 2006. They also drew attention to the fact that despite repeated recommendations from the Electoral Commision in 2003, 2004 and 2005 the government had not moved to change the law to prevent electoral fraud, the Electoral Administration Act being years late, ineffective and not meeting the recommendations the Commission had made.

The Council of Europe decided to appoint "rapporteurs" (reporters or investigators to you and me) to gather evidence to enable it to decide where to go from here.

Those chosen were Mrs Herta Dauber-Gmelin of Germany, a former Justice Minister and Senator Ursula Gacek of Poland, both experienced politicians and from the two largest groups in the European parliament, the Socialist group and the European People's Party respectively.

The UK government, in the meantime, was still expressing complete confidence in the integrity of the British electoral system. In March 2006 a minister had told Parliament "everyone agrees that electoral fraud is very rare".   In fact everyone agreed no such thing, which was why an investigation was called for.

At the request of Bridget Prentice, Parliamentary Under Secretary of State for Constitutional Affairs, who told the Council of Europe's investigators that the Electoral Administration Act had cleared up the previous problems with postal voting the two rapporteurs decided to delay making their report until after the local elections of 2007 – the first which would be held after the passing of the EAA 2006 – so that they could assess the effects of the legislation.

This done they forwarded their report to the Committee on the Honouring of Obligations and Commitments by Member States of the Council of Europe (Usually referred to as the Monitoring Committee, for obvious reasons.)

European Committees are inclined to be measured in their language and careful in their criticisms of member countries, especially large, relatively powerful, net contributors to the EU budget. Democratic norms are also something of a sensitive subject – few countries enjoy being criticised on these grounds and some of the accession states of Eastern Europe have only a brief experience of democracy in their entire history and much of that very recently. It would be miraculous if there were no flaws and for this reason the EU and its associated bodies tend to be tactful on the topic. The report therefore is interesting for what it is willing to say.

"From the findings of the rapporteurs, it is clear that the electoral system in Great Britain is open to electoral fraud. This vulnerability is mainly the result of the, rather arcane, system of voter registration without personal identifiers. It was exacerbated by the introduction of postal voting on demand, especially under the arrangements as existed before the changes in the electoral code in 2006. The 2006 changes to the electoral code enhanced the security of the postal voting arrangements, but other shortcomings and vulnerabilities remain.

Together with numerous British experts we strongly recommend to eliminate these.

Despite the vulnerabilities in the electoral system there is no doubt that elections in the United Kingdom are conducted democratically....It should be stressed however, that the United Kingdom delivers democratic elections despite the vulnerabilities in its electoral system. [original emphasis S.B.] These vulnerabilities could easily affect the overall democratic nature of elections in Great Britain. The Monitoring Committee should, in its periodic reports on the honouring of commitments by member states, pay special attention to electoral issues in the United Kingdom and, if the vulnerabilities noted are found to undermine the overall democratic nature of future elections in Great Britain, apply to initiate a Monitoring procedure with respect tothe United Kingdom." (Opinion for the Bureau of the Assembly prepared by the Committee on the Honouring of Obligations and Commitments by Member States of the Council of Europe www.assembly.coe.int/CommitteeDocs/2008/electoral_fraud-uk_E.pdf)

Elsewhere in the report it is made quite clear that it is "childishly simple for any person to fraudulently alter the [postal] vote especially in the light of the surprisingly laxrules governing altered ballot papers. The legal provisions that allow an altered ballot paper being treated as valid as long as the ballot shows the clear intention of the voter are an invitation to electoral fraud." (Paras 98 – 99)

The authors also remark "None of the 2006 changes in the Electoral Code addresses the ...opportunity for electoral fraud by means of bogus entries on the voters' list." (para 90) and "electoral fraud commited in this manner is very hard to detect." (para 89) "the combination of the household registration system without personal identifiers and the postal vote on demand arrangements make the electoral system in Great Britain very vulnerable to electoral fraud." The report also expresses great concern over "the fact that completed ballot packs can be legally handled by persons who do not have an official reason to do so, seriously undermines the principle of the secrecy of the vote."

The Electoral Commission had of course recommended that this be done away with but due to party pressure this principle, that activists should not take postal ballot packs, had become a guideline rather than a law which all three main parties then cheerfully ignored.

Discussing the Electoral Administration Act they say "most notable is what was not included in the changes to the electoral legislation. Despite explicit recommendations from many experts including the Electoral Commission and the Commission on Standards in Public Life, the government decided not to introduce a system of individual registration with personal identifiers, and decided to maintain the system of carrying forward names on the voters' list for one year if no new registration information has been forthcoming." (para 74)

(Although it should be noted that the Electoral Commission has expressed concerns that individual registration in Northern Ireland where it is standard since 2002 "may have had a negative impact on disadvantaged, hard to reach and marginalised groups – see the Electoral Commision's research report into the Electoral Fraud Northern Ireland Act)

Remarkably, even the limited confidence the report expresses in the EAA 2006 was before the Slough election petition exposed its failures – Election Commisioner Richard Mawrey said there were fourteen forms of fraud used at Birmingham and the EAA would only stop one of them. Roll stuffing, of course, he referred to as the fifteenth fraud (See Simmons v Khan). Nevertheless, despite its care to express confidence in British elections overall the report makes it clear that there is no guarantee that reasons for such confidence will continue.

The rapporteurs had also recommended that the Venice Commission be consulted as to whether the voter registration system and the way in which postal voting was carried out in the UK met Council of Europe Standards. They also asked that the Venice Commission should consider the legitimacy of the UK having very different voting rules for the mainland and Northern Ireland. In Northern Ireland there is a strict system of personal identifiers and much tighter controls on postal and proxy voting, introduced because of a widespread public perception that fraud was endemic in Northern Irish elections.

The Venice Commision's response did not go so far as saying that the UK failed to meet Council of Europe standards, although from it the

Monitoring Committee drew the conclusion that "the handling of postal ballots by third persons, who have no legal necessity to do so, such as party activists, *runs counter to Council of Europe standards.* [Emphasis added S.B.] The rapporteurs therefore strongly recommend to the British authorities to prohibit this practice for future elections." (para123)

The response of the Venice Commision was printed in full as Appendix One of the Monitoring Committee's report. It cited the fact that increasing voter turnout is a laudable aim in a democracy and praised the British government's introduction of sanctions for those attempting to vote fraudulently or steal another's vote.

However the report still contains some very serious caveats

"Certain inherent difficulties in postal, proxy or e-voting can never be completely overcome. The advantage and convenience to the electors, and therefore incidentally their contribution to the overall aim of greater voter participation, have to be balanced with the inevitable dangers and risks of these absent voting systems. One may doubt whether *de minimus* should be applied in electoral matters *a priori* . That is a political decision to be taken by each individual country. One realises, however, that if voting takes place in an unsupervised context, it is virtually impossible to guarantee that it will be carried out in secret, and that lack of secrecy constitutes a serious violation of the principles of freedom and fairness that govern elections in democratic states. This applies to proxy, postal or e-voting, that is, to all variations of absent voting." (para 43)

The report goes on to examine the system of absent voting in Northern Ireland with its strong controls and concludes that it is better in accord with the principles of the Council of Europe than the system used in the UK. It suggests the UK government might wish to consider extending it *to* the rest of the UK.

One thing they do not comment on specifically however is that, as they acknowledge above, there is always room for coercion in absent voting, secrecy not being guaranteed. In the context of Northern Ireland where so many of the political parties have access to weapons and well organised supporters willing to use them this is perhaps something that might have been looked at in more detail.

The full Opinion, with attendant appendices, was published in January 2008. The response of the British government, an answer to a Parliamentary question to Minister of State Bridget Prentice, was to say

"The government have noted the Committee's findings, and that it has not recommended opening a monitoring procedure with respect to the

United Kingdom. I understand that the opinion will now be considered by the Bureau of the Parliamentary Assembly of the Council of Europe, and the Government will await the outcome of the Bureau's consideration of the opinion before deciding whether it would be appropriate to issue a formal response to the opinion." (Hansard 10 March 2008) And there the matter rested. The government might reasonably have thought it had got off lightly although there was a degree of media comment that could not have made pleasant reading (e.g. Guardian, 22/01/2008 "Voting Open to 'childishly simple' fraud says watchdog").

A few weeks after that the papers were again filled with the Peterborough case where candidates had arranged for postal votes to be applied for and misdirected. This cannot have helped but undermine the confidence in the electoral system of any voters who saw it but the government could quite rightly claim that it had happened in 2004, long before the EAA 2006 had been passed.

Then , in the middle of the local election campaigns, another report was published and the whole issue flared up again.

This time the report came from the Joseph Rowntree Reform Trust. The JRRT is one of four trusts funded by the legacy of Joseph Rowntree, millionaire philanthropist and chocolate manufacturer, who left half his fortune for the purpose. The other three are concerned with issues such as charitable giving, the causes of deprivation and social exclusion and managing a stock of social housing.

On its website the Reform Trust states

"The Trust seeks to correct imbalances of power;

strengthening the hand of individuals, groups and organisations who are striving for reform;

foster democratic reform, civil liberties and social justice.

The Trust is not committed to the policies of any one political party although it has been a long term funder of the Liberal Democrats (and predecessor parties) in order to redress the balance of financial inequality between parties and to foster political developments central to a healthy democratic process. It has also supported individual politicians or groups promoting new ideas and policies from all the major parties in the UK." (www.jrrt.org.uk)

Despite being a source of funding for a political party the JRRT is a widely respected body. Nor did it simply have its own staff write a report

– it commissioned the equally well respected academic Stuart Wilks-Heeg of the University of Liverpool to carry out "an independent, evidence-based review...to establish the extent to which available evidence highlights potential threats to the integrity of UK elections." (JRRT Report Purity of Elections Executive Summary) assisted by two PhD students acting as researchers. Stuart Wilks-Heeg is also co-author of "Local Government from Thatcher to Blair: The Politics of Creative Autonomy" (Polity Press 2000) and "Whose Town Is It Anyway? The State of Local Democracy In Two Northern Towns" among others.

Like Mawrey's latest judgement the report concluded that "the reforms introduced by the Electoral Administration Act 2006 have proved deficient in combating electoral fraud, but also that the rationale for postal voting as a means of boosting turnout is likely to be fundamentally flawed."

However, unlike Mawrey who it might have been argued was seeing cases that were, by definition, untypical Wilks-Heeg was using a wide range of documentary evidence and a series of interviews with senior representatives of the Electoral Commision, the Association of Electoral Administrators and the Association of Chief Police Officers, among others.

(The report also had a section on the targeting of marginal seats with large sums of campaigning money, which is not strictly relevant to this book)

The JRRT report cited an estimated minimum of forty-two convictions for electoral offences since the 2000 Act that introduced postal voting on demand, but also warned that there had been relatively little research on this and estimated "the actual number of prosecutions for electoral offences is likely to be at least double that recorded in official statistics." (pp 31)

It goes on to argue

"There are three ways in which we might seek to interpret this data on electoral offences since 2000. The first interpretation, put forward by the Electoral Commission, is that proven cases of fraud and malpractice relate to a tiny proportion of the elections held since 2000" (pp 32) It is absolutely true that only 0.1 per cent of all candidates in the period were ever convicted of anything – a powerful argument for the opinion of the Council of Europe rapporteurs that UK elections were still free and fair.

"A second, counter interpretation, however, would be that the number of convictions reflects the difficulties of securing sufficient evidence to prosecute...several senior police officers have suggested that figures on current convictions clearly under-estimate the incidence of malpractice (Thames Valley Police, 2005; Metropolitan Police Authority, 2006). The third way of interpreting the available evidence is to focus... on what is revealed.. by the events documented in these cases... the interpretation of the issues ...advanced by legal scholars and academics has been unanimous in arguing that it reveals significant, *generic* weaknesses in the electoral system that have made it significantly more vulnerable to organised, large-scale fraud (Watt, 2006)." (pp 32)

What is *certain* is that every single police force in England except the City of London police (a small body covering the ancient City, not to be confused with the Metropolitan Police which covers the rest of London) submitted evidence to the Crown Prosecution Service concerning electoral offences between 2000 and 2006.

The report also looks at allegations of *biraderi* networks asserting themselves in British politics. Biraderi politics, groups of voters from certain areas and/or extended families voting en bloc is common practice in some parts of the Indian sub-continent, where it supplies a way for communities to maximise their political strength in situations where the location of a new government project can literally make the difference between life and death. The downside, of course, is that by putting the votes of large numbers of people in the hands of a few it entrenches existing hierarchies, and in order to work most effectively it needs those promising the delivery of voting blocs to be able to *guarantee* how people will vote. Salma Yaqoob, a Birmingham City Councillor and leading member of Respect has said

"It is for the reasons that biraderi (extended clan) networks can exert undue influence that we have been campaigning vigorously in Birmingham against postal votes. Women in particular have been disenfranchised. Postal votes are filled out in the 'privacy' of one's own home. But it is not private when family members, candidates or supporters, can influence – subtly or otherwise – the way you complete your vote...A secret ballot means that loyalties to family and friends can be maintained in public, but political arguments can still win out in the real privacy of the voting booth." (Socialist Renewal 02/01/2007).

It should be noted of course that without the secret ballot the voters are laid open not only to the relatively benevolent attentions of leaders who genuinely wish the best for their communities but believe themselves better qualified than anyone else to judge that best, but to out and out heavies and gangsters. The report also, rightly emphasises that its evidence on biraderi is primarily anecdotal. However the "anecdotes" are coming from experienced campaigners and politicians in the relevant communities rather than from the ignorant or those motivated by racist malice.

The JRRT report also expressed serious concerns about the decline in public confidence in the fairness of the electoral process suggesting that rates of confidence in the UK are the lowest in a list of ten European democracies surveyed. (The fact that successful convictions for electoral offences have not been confined to any one party but have covered all three main Westminister parties, Plaid Cymru, the BNP and the Democratic Unionist Party may be a factor in this.)

Like Mr Justice Mawrey the report concluded that "The provisions introduced by the Electoral Administration Act 2006 fall far short of what is required to ensure that electoral malpractice is kept to an absolute minimum...There have been numerous instances in which problems arising from the administration and management of elections have come close to leaving electoral outcomes open to challenge...There is a near universal consensus among electoral administrators that, had an election been called for November 2007, significant administrative problems would have arisen, perhaps on a scale that could have raised questions about the legitimacy of the election result." (JRRT Executive Summary pp5)

As we shall see these concerns have not gone away. The whole world *is* watching. If we don't put our own house in order foreign election monitors may yet be racking up frequent flier miles to the UK.

The Light At The End Of The Tunnel Might Not Be A Train Coming In The Other Direction – The Political Parties and Elections Act of 2009

On the 21st July 2009 the government took a giant step forward – and not over the edge of the precipice. In a hugely encouraging move the Political Parties and Elections Act 2009, amongst a number of administrative alterations and reforms, finally provided for a Northern Ireland style system of identifiers for voters. As we have seen this was strongly recommended by the Council of Europe rapporteurs, the Joseph Rowntree Reform Trust's report and the Electoral Commission. The Act also increases the powers of the Secretary of State in relation to establishing a CORE (Co-ordinated Online Record of Electors) scheme, which would do much to prevent voters being registered in different electoral areas at the same time.

It also extended the responsibilities of the Electoral Commission to issue guidance on best practice, gave it the right to impose a range of civil penalties such as fines and increased its investigatory powers. That said it also allowed for the appointment of up to four Commissioners from the political parties, following consultation with any party with two or more members in the House of Commons (This last presumably a deliberate attempt to annoy George Galloway, then the sole Respect MP).

Each political party may have no more than one Commissioner, guaranteeing that there will be a representative from outside the three main parties, almost certainly either some variety of Unionist from Northern Ireland or one of the various Celtic nationalist parties.

For our purposes however, the most important part of the Act was the introduction of personal identifiers for absent voting. In addition to the signature already required, voters wishing to register will now have to provide a National Insurance number and date of birth.

As the mere fact that identity theft is reckoned to be a severe problem in the UK demonstrates, it is by no means impossible for crooks to get hold of or manufacture this sort of information, and there will be those who can obtain it legitimately who will still not be entitled to vote in UK elections. Nevertheless no one can deny that this represents an enormous increase in the difficulties facing vote riggers and thus an enormous benefit to the rest of us. Is this then the solution? Has this book and the events it describes become a historical curiosity?

Unfortunately not.

There are a number of important caveats to be aware of. The first, and by far the most glaring, is that the new rules did *not come into force at all until the first of July, 2010 – after the 2010 General Election.*

The second is that *adhering to these rules will be completely voluntary until 2015 at the earliest – and they will only then come into force if Parliament chooses to make it so.* It is entirely possible that this will be after the date of the *next* General Election. The new coalition government has spoken of speeding up the process but so far no specifics have been fixed, and other, and controversial, priorities loom. Nor is there a guarantee the coalition will survive. It is impossible for anyone to predict the composition or attitude of Parliament in two or three years time.

Lastly, and more importantly than even the other two put together, these postal ballots *WILL STILL NOT BE SECRET.*

This is a vital point, one which cannot be stressed too much. The existence of a secret ballot is an essential guarantee that our elections are free. If ballots are not secret, voters can be threatened by gangsters, landlords, employers, councils, they can be put under pressure by relatives, friends, political activists, they can be discriminated against, they can be bribed, they can offer to sell their votes to the highest bidder. Article 25 of the International Covenant on Civil and Political Rights, a UN convention to which Britain is a signatory states explicitly "Every citizen shall have the right and the opportunity...to vote and to be elected at genuine periodic elections which shall be by universal and equal suffrage *and shall be held by secret ballot,* guaranteeing the free expression of the will of the electors." [emphasis added –S.B.]

As long as absent voting can take place without any real reason being required the UK is not meeting the obligations of that Covenant and never will.

The Sealed Ballot Box That Wasn't

In May 2008 in the Higher Blackley ward of Manchester BNP candidate Derek Adams spent the morning of the count checking the seals on ballot boxes in each polling station. Paranoid, most people will think. In this case however it turned out to be a very functional paranoia – when polling box 130 arrived at the count the seals had been changed.

Understandably perturbed, Mr Adams called an election official over and following an exchange of views, referred the matter to the Returning Officer and Chief Executive of Manchester City Council, Sir Howard Bernstein, who ruled that the count should go ahead.

Mr Adams subsequently wrote a letter of complaint and received a reply on 28th May 2008. This reply stated, quite correctly, that ballot boxes, before the election, are filled with "books of ballot papers, corresponding numbers' lists, registers, seals, signs and notices and other miscellaneous equipment" and sealed before being transported to the polling stations.

So far so good. Sir Howard's letter *then* went on to say "The Presiding Officer (PO) collected the ballot box and on arrival at the polling station managed to empty the box of all items without removing the seals that had been placed on the box for overnight storage. ...Then at some time between 8am and 9am the Polling Station Inspector (PSI) arrived at St Clare's to be informed by the Presiding

Officer (PO) that the ballot box was not tightly sealed. The PSI realised what the PO had done and telephoned the elections office for advice. The PSI was advised, with the PO, to refit the top of the ballot box and reseal the ballot box correctly and explain to any candidates or agents present what was happening and why. It was at this point that the correct seals were used on the ballot box....I am fully satisfied that although the Presiding Officer did not follow the correct procedure, the ballot box was secure at all times, from the opening of the poll at 7am to the delivery of the ballot box to the count."

The BNP did not believe a word of it. They published Sir Howard's letter on their website, strongly implied foul play and compared UK elections with those in Zimbabwe. It is not necessary to agree with them to be disturbed by this episode. The fact is that the items listed could not possibly be removed from a ballot box that was in any way secure. Taking the most optimistic possible view then, on the basis of the Presiding Officer and PSI's own accounts, the ballot box was effectively unsealed for between one and two hours. The Chief Executive's assurances are therefore meaningless – he knows that the security of the ballot box *was* breached and has no way of demonstrating that no one took advantage of this. To dismiss this as trivial is to undermine the security of elections as a whole – if we dismiss one incident as trivial why not all?

Sir Howard finished by saying "I will ensure that these issues are specifically addressed in future training sessions" Let us hope that the gravity of the issues, and not just the details are also covered.

The GLA Elections of 2008 and Scottish Elections of May 2007 – E-counting on trial

As we have seen in the earlier chapter on e-voting enough problems came up with the e-voting trials that no future experiments are currently planned. E counting, however, survived to be used in two important elections – the Scottish Parliamentary elections of 2007 and the Greater London Authority elections of 2008. There was some very considerable publicity around the Scottish elections, mainly because of a very large number of ballots which the electronic counting system proved unable to read, leading to serious delays in getting the results.

There was probably also confusion, with many members of the public believing that votes rejected by the e-counting system were treated as "spoilt" votes, and as such not counted. In fact such votes were re-examined by election staff, candidates and agents and where a clear intention could be established they were counted as valid.

This public perception was exacerbated by the fact that there were an unusually large number of spoilt ballots in the Scottish elections. In sixteen Scottish Parliamentary constituencies the number of spoilt ballots was greater than the winning candidate's margin of victory. Both the Open Rights Group (www.openrightsgroup.org/wp-content/uploads/org_exec_summary.pdf) and the Gould Report commissioned by the Electoral Commission blamed

this on the decision to combine elections for the Scottish Parliament and Scottish local authorities. This led to voters simultaneously marking ballot papers for two different electoral systems and having to make two crosses in two different columns for the Parliamentary election, one for their constituency candidate and one for their choice of party in the regional top-up seats.

The ORG believed the design of the ballot paper for the Scottish Parliament was a major source of confusion and criticised both the Electoral Commission and the government for not testing the design more thoroughly.

"It is ORG's view that the ballot design unfairly penalised smaller parties which only stood regional candidates."

(See the ORG executive summary at the web address above.) The Gould report took an equally critical view. The ORG also noted that it was the decision of the Scottish Executive and the Scotland Office to run the two elections simultaneously – it was not imposed upon them. The Gould report described " a notable level of party self interest evident in Ministerial decision making (especially in regard to the timing and method of counts and the design of ballot papers)." (Gould pp 17)

The biggest problem the Open Rights Group found with the e-counting however, was the fact that it almost changed the result of the whole Scottish Parliamentary election.

The final regional result to be declared was for the Highlands and Islands area with seven Parliamentary seats.

"During the adjudication process, Mr Thompson [now an SNP Member of the Scottish Parliament S. B.] had been keeping an informal count which led him to believe that the SNP was receiving approximately 35% of the votes for additional members (the regional list). However when the RO presented the regional results to candidates and agents prior to declaration, SNP representatives were shocked and disappointed to have not won any seats." (ORG op cit)

After a brief consultation with his agent Mr Thompson decided to challenge the result and managed to intercept the RO on his way to officially announce the results. (Had he not managed to do so of course it would have taken legal action to overturn the declaration, even if everybody, RO included had immediately seen and acknowledged the error.)

The RO agreed to show Mr Thompson the data from which the result had been calculated and discovered that votes for the SNP had not been included at all in the totals "probably owing to the spreadsheet operator's inability to see all the parties' votes on the computer screen at the same time." (ORG op cit)

Apologising profusely the RO recalculated the results with all the parties' votes included, giving the SNP two seats across the region, thus making it the largest party in the Scottish Parliament, just one ahead of Labour. None of this constitutes fraud, of course but it has the same effect in depriving voters of their democratic choice and indicates an uncertainty and difficulty in the counting process that would certainly make the task of vote stealers easier. One simple evidence of the pressures election staff, candidates and agents were working under was that some of them had been awake and working for thirty-five hours at the time the mistaken results were almost announced.

Although they did not spot any fraud however, the ORG observers did find a number of factors which potentially laid the count open to fraud. Firstly the traditional metal ballot boxes were not used; instead there were a wide mouthed flat pack plastic kind. "Observers as well as candidates and agents interviewed raised concerns about whether the boxes and their seals were robust enough to prevent ballot stuffing after the close of polls." (ORG op cit). They were certainly not robust enough to stand up to assault as a member of the public was helpful enough to demonstrate by attacking a polling place in Edinburgh with a golf club (ORG op cit & Gould).

The reason for the new ballot boxes was so that voters could place their marked ballots inside without folding them as unfolded ballot papers were easier to scan and did not have creases which the scanners might interpret as additional markings requiring adjudication but this did mean that it would be possible for a voter's choice to be visible as they walked from the polling booth to the ballot box. Some concerns were expressed about this. (ORG op cit)

"ORG observers noted that the DRS vote-scanning machines had open, unguarded USB parallel and serial ports available...In general observers noted good security...however..the open ports do present a security risk. Given the number of scanners (32 observed in Glasgow alone), the number of people attending counts and the length of time for which the counts extended it would be a simple matter for unauthorised individuals to gain access to one or more of these ports enabling the manipulation or loading of software...Due to the systems being networked compromise of one system can lead to compromise of all computers at a count location. " (ORG op cit)

Furthermore, the report added "candidates and agents at all counts observed in Scotland frequently raised questions about how the accuracy of the count could be confirmed. No sample manual recounts were required at counts observed...It is unclear how one could have detected software manipulations or errors that maintained the total of votes counted but changed to whom they were cast." (ORG op cit) ORG considered the conduct and reliability of the Scottish elections superior to the English e-voting pilots but again "given the problems observed and the questions remaining unanswered" (ORG op cit) could not declare its confidence in the results.

The London elections of 2008 involved an electorate of almost five and a half million – that is to say, greater than the entire population of Scotland. The people of London were voting for a Mayor, fourteen constituency members of the Greater London Authority elected by the traditional first past the post system and for party lists which would elect another eleven members of the Authority on the 'top up' or Additional Member System (AMS). The voting ystem for the authority is the same as that for the Scottish Parliament or the Welsh Assembly. The Mayor, however, is elected on the Single Transferrable Vote system, with voters listing their choices in order of preference 1, 2, 3, until they run out of interest or candidates they wish to vote for. If no candidate wins an overall majority in the first round of voting then lower ranking candidates are eliminated and their voters' second preferences istributed until eventually a winner emerges. Unlike the Scottish elections of a year before three separate ballot papers were issued, one for each different kind of vote.

The Electoral Commission's report on the GLA elections praised aspects of the election saying

"The implementation of electronic counting at the 2008 GLA elections was better planned and executed than many previous experiences across England, Scotland and Wales. The team responsible for planning and managing the electronic counting element of the London elections had clearly learned a great deal from the 2000 and 2004 GLA elections, from the experience of the Scottish elections in 2007 and from the smaller pilot schemes at local elections since 2000."

(www.
Electoralcommission.org.uk/_data/assets/pdf_file/0005/57857/GLA-
Elections-Report-2008-revised.pdf) but then went on to say

"Nevertheless, we are extremely concerned that neither the
Commission nor our technical advisers have been given access to the
full reports of the independent testing commissioned by the GLRO
[Greater London Returning Officer – S. B.] Given the technical nature of
electronic systems which are used to deliver elements of the election
process, both electors and candidates (as well as political parties) are
increasingly reliant on effective independent audit to provide such
assurance. We recognise that commercial suppliers....may wish to
protect their commercial interests. However, such wishes should never
take priority over the interests of electors and other participants.."
(Electoral Commission op cit).

Certainly if the Electoral Commission, the government body whose job
it is to monitor the proper conduct of elections cannot get access to key
information it cannot help but be worrying. ORG observers were even
more critical stating that "On the day of the count, efforts towards
transparency around the recording of valid votes were nothing more than
pretence, As a result, many ORG observers concluded that they were
unable to observe valid votes being recorded. The hundreds of screens
set up by the scanners showed almost meaningless data to observers,
party candidates and agents.." (Open Rights Group May 2008 Election
Report)

Some observers might be even more worried by the fact that the
company providing the e-counting was Indra. Acute readers will
remember that Indra was the company that ran the pilot e counting
system in the elections at Dereham the previous year. They will also
remember that those elections descended into utter chaos. In the one
ward where a manual re-count took place (Dereham-Humbletoft) 56.1
per cent of all votes had been missed by e-counting and in another ward
two hundred and twenty-one more votes had been cast than should
have been while the checksum digit either didn't exist or didn't work.

London Elects stated, quite correctly, that tests had been done in 2007
to check that the same result was obtained with a manual and an

electronic count, however "It emerged in later meetings with London Elects that the manual counts had been repeated until the number of votes counted manually matched the number counted electronically" (ORG op cit) which is not quite the same thing as ensuring accuracy. Both the Electoral Commission and the ORG expressed regret that no statistical sample manual counts were taken at the time of the election.

Another problem that set alarm bells ringing was concern over the ballot boxes and their seals. As we have seen, the fact of ballot boxes being tamper proof is an important guarantee against ballot box stuffing. In this election however the ballot boxes were constructed not out of metal or even plastic but from white cardboard boxes 'sealed' with small purple sticky labels provided by the GLRO's office.

"However, a significant number of the seals became unstuck during both polling day and overnight due to their small size, failure to adhere under pressure from the thick cardboard flap and flexing of the boxes during transport." (Electoral Commission op cit)

Significant is certainly the word. A disgruntled BNP, convinced that it had been stitched up, published a photo on its website of rows and rows of ballot boxes hanging open with seals dangling. Whatever one thinks of the BNP and my views are both clear and extraordinarily anti they were surely right in concluding that this would have received far more publicity in Zimbabwe – in fact it got almost none at all. The ORG also noted that some seals had been incorrectly applied so that boxes could have been opened from the bottom without the top seals being disturbed.

The Electoral Commission, oddly, stated "We have seen no evidence that the apparently poor quality of ballot box seals led to any malpractice or impropriety." (Electoral Commission op cit) Oddly, because unsealed ballot boxes *are* evidence, albeit not proof positive, of malpractice or impropriety. If they are to be ignored then anyone with access to the box, blank ballots and a marked register can add votes completely undetectably and with ballot boxes being stored overnight would have had hours to do so.

Even without blank ballots and a register, votes cast could easily be spoiled. A full examination of whether the "turn out" or the average number of spoiled ballot papers coming out of all or some of the unsealed ballot boxes was higher than average might have provided valuable pointers and/or helped to restore confidence but this does not appear to have been done, and to be fair there are immense difficulties which would have stood in the way of any individual or body trying to do so. The Commission was disturbed enough to recommend that

 "The quality and suitability of ballot boxes and seals needs to be considered by the GLRO in the light of this experience." (Electoral Commission op cit)

 Things could theoretically be worse however. If discrepancies in the number of votes that were supposed to be in a ballot box were ignored then another major safeguard would be gone – coupled with the broken seals it would mean that any number of votes could be added without let or hindrance.

 Unfortunately, this is exactly what happened next.

 Forty- eight percent of all ballot boxes had a discrepancy between the number of ballots that were recorded as being in them and the number that came out. Discrepancies of one or two ballots are by no means unknown as tired staff under pressure make slight mistakes and more than half of the forty-eight per cent fell into this category – fencepost errors, as they are known. However nineteen per cent contained discrepancies of more than three votes, and two per cent , eighty-eight ballot boxes, contained discrepancies of more than one hundred votes. (Electoral Commission op cit).

Neither of the reports makes it clear how many, if any, of these were also ballot boxes with open seals.

 According to the ORG the margin of variance in two constituency seats was greater than the margin of victory of the winning candidates. ORG also rightly notes that there are possible innocent explanations involving electors taking ballot papers home, scanning errors etc and then goes into some moderately complicated calculations as to exactly how many ballots were counted but not issued, coming up with possible figures ranging from 301 to 41, 213, which rather proves their next point, that clearly the ballot box verification process as a means of checking accuracy was "deeply flawed" (ORG op cit).

The Electoral Commission's report stated (in bold) "We have significant concerns about the number and size of discrepancies between the numbers of ballot papers expected and the numbers verified as having been scanned...we think it is unlikely that such apparently high verification discrepancies would be acceptable to the majority of Returning Officers. It is possible, as we acknowledge above, that most or all of these verification discrepancies can be explained, but the electronic counting system used at these elections did not support the more detailed notes that might provide an audit trail of individual decisions or corrections...which is usual in a manual count." (Electoral Commission op cit)

Come the actual counting of the ballots the huge number (more than four hundred thousand) which were initially rejected and sent to adjudication is well known. Almost as

well known is the fact that scanners were picking up creases, ink spots a specks of dust on screens as markings, so that valid votes were being re-examined, at a huge cost in time and effort, because there was a crease or spot by the name of a second candidate. Less well known are some of the other problems observers spotted.

For example, ORG concluded that blank ballots must be being recorded as votes where a speck of ink or dirt was against one candidate's name. This is not fraud but tends towards the same effect – making real votes worthless. Problems in the adjudication process had the same effect.

"ORG received a report from a party agent that he had seen a valid vote for another party rejected at second-level adjudication stage. The agent reported that adjudication decisions were happening so fast that he could not challenge the adjudicators until after they had clicked "Accept". The adjudicators, having been challenged on this decision, attempted to go back and change the decision, but found that they were unable to. Indra were called over to try and fix things, but they were unable to bring the ballot back into the adjudication queue to have the adjudication decision changed. The agent was told by the CRO that the vote would be recorded as being lost due to administrative error." (ORG op cit)

Why anyone should lose their vote in a free country because "the computer says no" was not, apparently, explained. Both ORG and the Electoral Commission saw other examples of voters being disenfranchised due to the IT system.

Also, almost a fortnight after the election the GLRO had to write to the election agents for the Mayoral candidates explaining that some votes had not been correctly transmitted, reducing Boris Johnson's majority by 132 votes. If this error took two weeks to be spotted what else could have been missed? (Election Commission op cit)

Unsurprisingly the Open Rights Group concluded that there were enough errors and not enough transparency for it to conclude whether the results declared were accurate. It also recommended against repeating or extending elections with e-counting unless a set of safety measures improving transparency and accuracy were not only introduced but proven to be more cost effective than a manual count.

The Electoral Commission did not go so far as that but it did express a number of caveats, some of which are quoted above. The other key ones were that there should be a full cost-benefit analysis of manual versus electronic counting and the second was that there should be no more e-counting until a series of major steps, including altering the law to guarantee transparency had been carried out. The Commission goes over a number of important flaws noted and states "we would start from the assumption that the 2012 GLA elections would be counted manually" adding "Any assessment of the costs and benefits of using electronic counting should include an assessment of the impact of electronic counting on the scrutiny role of candidates and observers, and on broader public confidence in the effectiveness and integrity of the counting of votes."

The information outlined above should make it clear that the danger of e-counting is that it is by no means more reliable or faster than human beings but is certainly more opaque – fraud or error is far harder to detect or reverse.

Since the Electoral Commission's report was published there have been two more developments on this topic. Firstly an official report has been published saying that e-counting for GLA elections will cost £1.5 million pounds more than a manual count. (Guardian 30/09/2009) The ORG thinks even this report overestimates the costs of a manual count.

Secondly the Chief Executive of the GLA has decided to go ahead with e-counting for the 2012 elections anyway.

Glengarry, Glenrothes

On the 6th November 2008 a Parliamentary by-election for the seat of Glenrothes in central Scotland took place. It came not long after a painful defeat for Labour at the hands of the Scottish National Party (SNP) in the Glasgow East by-election on 24th July 2008 and at a time when the government was scoring low in the polls. Labour supporters were therefore pleasantly surprised when they won. (although the fact that this was seen as something of a triumph in what was traditionally a rock-solid Labour area indicates just how low the party's expectations had become.)   In contrast to the Glasgow East by election, where the swing from Labour to SNP was 22.6 per cent at Glenrothes it was less than five per cent.

On 19th November however, apparently slightly disconcerted at the loss and at the fact that Labour's votes cast actually went up overall by several hundred votes AND as a percentage of votes cast the runner up SNP officially enquired the cost of a copy of the marked register and the marked register of postal voters.
(www.scots.courts.gov.uk/docs/report/Report_Investigation_Into_Missing_Electoral_Register2009.pdf)

According to the official report, available at the internet address above, "despite reminders, that request was not pursued until late January 2009. [By which time it would have been far too late to bring an election petition, whatever evidence of wrongdoing was found S.B.] The marked register of electors was reported as missing in the last week of January 2009...During the investigation it was established that the marked register ..of postal voters, ..the ballot paper accounts, rejected papers and verification sheets were also missing."

Without those registers there was no possible way of telling if the votes counted at the by-election related to those cast by voters. As the earlier chapter on "The Mechanics of Voting and Vote Rigging" details, it is the first safeguard against the stuffing of ballot boxes. (This was not the first time a marked register had gone missing – the registers in Woking had vanished after the 2005 elections, - see Hansard 30/06/2005 - leading to the Labour and Liberal Democrat groups putting down a motion for the council to employ an extra officer specifically to combat electoral fraud, allegations of which had hit the borough in 2004 and 2005)

An SNP Member of the Scottish Parliament, Tricia Marwick rightly said "In the absence of these documents it is impossible for anyone to say if this was a fair or unfair election." (The Courier 06/03/2009) It was also a clear breach of the legal responsibilities of those involved. In Scotland at the time this was the Sherriff's clerks, although responsibility was transferred to the Returning Officer in 2010. For this reason, the Sheriffs' Clerks and Court Service being the responsibility of the SNP led Scottish government, one Labour MSP said the entire debacle was the fault of the SNP itself – the party that had actually brought the scandal to light. Claire Baker MSP added "While the election result was never seriously in question it is important that the electoral process is as transparent and open as possible."(Courier 06/03/2009) While agreeing heartily with the sentiments concerning openness and transparency it has to be said that without the missing documents no one can say whether the process was ever in doubt – that is the point of them.

Worryingly, the Electoral Commission's report (as opposed to the Scottish Court Service's report) devotes a grand total of one paragraph to this incident.

The official court services report does specifically say that no evidence of malice in the disappearance of the records was found. Unfortunately, no evidence of anything was found which was pretty much the problem. The report was unable to say how literally dozens of bags and boxes of information had disappeared without trace. It also emerged that it was impossible to reconstruct the marked register without a formal order from either the House of Commons or a Court.

That Commons order was given, and reconstruction commenced on 16th November 2009. Unfortunately at that late stage, investigators would have been unable to combine it with enough other information to construct a case if wrongdoing *had* taken place.

It should be stressed that it is entirely possible that the turnout and the poll-defying Labour vote and the increased number of postal votes applied for (more than six thousand) and the disappearance of thousands of pages of public information are nothing more than a series of extraordinary coincidences. Certainly it would be entirely wrong to suggest wrongdoing by any individual or group or supporters of any party without much, much firmer evidence and certainly it would have to be a very, very blatant crook willing to dispose of the multiple sacks of election info that went missing.

What cannot be denied is that any election without a marked register of voters and postal voters, freely available for inspection cannot be proven to be free and fair and as such would not meet international standards.

The 2010 General Election: Night of The Long Lines

Although (unlike 2005) it was spared an ongoing court case for electoral fraud during the campaign the General Election of 2010 still had an air of déjà vu for anyone who had taken an interest in vote rigging over the previous few years.

Craig Murray, former British Ambassador to Uzbekistan again devoted his time to making Jack Straw's life difficult. Although not a candidate this time round he enthusiastically backed independent candidate Bushra Irfa for Jack Straw's Blackburn seat. Writing in the Guardian newspaper he told the world that local election officials had refused to allow Ms Irfa to place her own seals on the ballot box on the grounds that there wasn't enough room. (Guardian 08/04/2010)

If this allegation was true the officials would, of course, have been breaking the law: candidates have been entitled to add their own seals to the ballot box since the nineteenth century. However, given what has happened in London and Manchester, with election officials ignoring broken seals and carrying on regardless (see previous chapters) it might not have made a difference anyway.

The same questions of treating, the unlawful provision of free food and drink to voters by candidates and their agents arose again in Blackburn in exactly the same way.

According to Craig Murray's blog free food was given to voters at a Jack Straw rally in Blackburn on the 25th April. Subsequently, so Murray states, the local police issued a formal warning to Mr Straw's election agent not to do it again. The arguments around this approach I have covered fairly comprehensively in the chapter on the 2005 election, but Mr Murray must have felt vindicated when the serving of food was cancelled at a later election rally "as it would be against electoral law" and much of the audience got up and left.

(http://www.craigmurray.org.uk/archives/2010/05/jack_thwarted)

Elsewhere the Evening Standard was reprising its role from 2005 when it went round London finding ghost voters – fictional characters on the electoral register almost certainly placed there by vote riggers so postal votes can be applied for in their names. As in 2005 journalists found examples ridiculously easy to discover.

"The Standard found two homes in Bethnal Green where, respectively, eight and ten apparent ghost voters with Muslim names are registered for postal votes. In fact only five people live at the two properties and they know nothing of the 18 other people listed there.

"At a house in Bow 18 postal ballots were delivered yesterday but only 10 of the voters named live there. They say a Bengali-speaking man came to the door two weeks ago and told them they had to sign forms." (Evening Standard 30/04/2010)

The article also quoted unnamed politicians as saying that activists had been visiting homes and offering to post ballots for the vulnerable or "assist" voters in filling out their postal ballot forms. Both practices are of course a breach of the Electoral Commission's code of practice, but NOT against the law, meaning there is little anyone can do about it. The reason they are not against the law is that the then Government ignored the Commission's recommendations and as we have seen all three parties have cheerfully ignored the code of practice ever since. Like the rules on MPs' expenses the law on postal ballots allows clearly unethical actions to go unpunished because it was written by the same people who stand to benefit from those actions.

Meanwhile, in Derby, police were investigating allegations that intimidation had been used to persuade voters to voters to cast postal ballots for the Labour Party. (Derby Telegraph 28/04/2010) Of course, if there were no postal ballots all the intimidation in the world couldn't influence a voter because their vote would be secret, a fact that has been repeatedly pointed out since postal voting on demand began, to no avail. The investigations were dropped due to insufficient evidence, which may be a sign of squeaky clean politics in Derby or may simply be yet more proof that electoral fraud is notoriously difficult to stop as long as the laws that make it possible remain in place.

In the London borough of Tower Hamlets 5,166 names were added to the Electoral Register just before the deadline on 20 April. (Mail 04/05/2010) Some will have been real people, genuinely entitled to vote but others will almost certainly have been ghost voters. Naturally there is no possible way officials could check up on that many names so close to an election, a fact vote riggers know and rely on. In Birmingham in 2004 the number of late registrations and late applications for postal votes was one of the key factors leading to the overwhelming of the Returning Officer's team.

To give some idea of the scale of the checking problem it is estimated that at least seven million names were registered for a postal vote in the 2010 General Election (Commonwealth Observer Team Final Report). A few tens of thousands in the right seats would have been more than enough to swing the whole election – *not more than one per cent of postal votes cast needed to be fraudulent to rig the whole election – just so long as they were in the right place.*

In fact marginal seats in many places showed a dramatic rise in the number of postal votes cast. For example, the marginal areas of Edinburgh South and Barnet saw an increase in postal votes of around sixty per cent. (Mail 04/05/2010)

Back in Tower Hamlets Jerome Taylor a journalist for the Independent noticed that the number of adults registered to vote at the home of Labour council candidate Khales Uddin Ahmed had jumped from five to twelve in the space of a few weeks. This is of course not proof of any wrongdoing but interested him enough that he thought it worth going to see Mr Ahmed who, alas, refused to speak to him.

So far, so nothing. There is no reason why anyone should speak to a journalist and it is entirely possible that seven friends, relatives or lodgers should move into a council candidate's already somewhat crowded home and make a point of registering to vote

shortly before an important election. (Although the Election Court in Slough was profoundly unconvinced by a similar claim re the 'Walthamstow Six'). Then Mr Taylor was assaulted and beaten in broad daylight just a few yards from Mr Uddin's home after being approached by a group of youths . Still nothing, East London is not and never has been a safe area. However the man who rescued Mr Taylor maintains he saw two of the youths flee into Mr Uddin's property. (Independent 04/05/2010) Police interviewed at least three Labour candidates in the borough over claims of electoral fraud in the run-up to the election. (Independent 05/05/2010) A "senior Labour source" told Channel Four News that the party had been assured that relatives had indeed recently moved in to live with Mr Uddin.
(http://www.channel4.com/news/articles/uk/vote+rigging+claims+rai se+electoral+questions/3636102)

At the other end of London in the suburb of Southall the Times found twenty-seven voters registered to a small flat above a florist which belonged to the family of an independent council candidate. Mr Dalawar Chaudry had been deselected by Labour after he was found employing illegal immigrants in his restaurant.

"Chaudry said the properties were rented out and he had no knowledge of the voters 'I am as gobsmacked as you...a lot of people live in Southall' he said" (Times 09/05/2010) Fifteen of the voters had been added in the month before the general election and Mr Chaudry and his family owned two other properties in the constituency with a further twenty-four registered voters, most of them also having been added in recent weeks. Just to prove that the renting out of intensely crowded properties was not simply a Labour habit the Times also found a Conservative candidate, Mr Avtar Singh Kaira with an average of fourteen voters registered at each of the three properties he owned or co-owned.

Mr Khaira said "..People are always coming and going." (Times 09/05/2010).

It should be noted that this does not constitute any proof of wrongdoing on the part of either of these gentlemen but does show

how little control or monitoring of the electoral register exists. (Both candidates lost their elections so if, unbeknownst to them, a criminal mastermind was vote rigging on their behalf he/she wasn't doing it very well.)

On 1st May the BBC reported from Mirpur in Pakistan where there are large numbers of British or dual British/Pakistani citizens. The area has had strong links with the UK for decades. Many men from the area served with the British Indian Army, fighting in two World Wars and in the sixties a dam was built that flooded much of the local farmland, causing dispossessed farmers to flock to Britain in search of work. UK citizens here are entitled to vote by post or proxy in British elections.

(For those who question why people not living in the UK, not paying its taxes or being affected by its social conditions should be allowed to help choose its future in this way, this particular right was granted in the 1983 Representation of the People Act by Margaret Thatcher's government and was widely denounced at the time as a plot to allow the Conservatives to tap into the votes of wealthy expatriates. If it was, it has clearly fallen victim to the law of unintended consequences.)

There is therefore nothing illegal or underhand in the fact that canvassers have been working hard to gain the support of British citizens living here. What *is* both a clear breach of the Electoral Commission's Code of Practice and an open goal for vote riggers is that they have reportedly persuaded voters to simply sign proxy voting forms giving their votes to others. One man explained to the BBC how it was done.

"...people are going door to door asking Britons to blindly sign proxy voting forms for the upcoming elections, allowing someone else in the UK to vote on their behalf. 'They said I didn't have to fill in any details, just to sign my name at the bottom of the form,' he says smiling. "So I signed two."

He laughed as he told me he had no idea who was going to vote on his behalf, and whom they were going to vote for.

"I personally know 25 other people who did the same thing, lots of people just on this street, but everybody does it."

Many others, among the contingent of thousands of British citizens thought to be here, have admitted signing proxy forms in this way"

(http://news.bbc.co.uk/1/hi/uk_politics/election_2010/8655697.stm)

The dangers are obvious. Even if a voter did know who would be casting the proxy vote on his/her behalf and gave them instructions on how to cast it there is absolutely no guarantee they will follow those instructions and no way to tell if they have done so. Equally, how are the UK authorities supposed to check signatures from individuals living many thousands of miles away in one of the world's key trouble spots? (Mirpur district is part of Kashmir which has been disputed between India and Pakistan since the nineteen-forties, a source of constant tension and intermittent armed conflict.)

Even worse, it is impossible for the British authorities to guarantee that proxy and postal votes have been cast without coercion or intimidation from within the UK – in Mirpur, where UK law has no jurisdiction there is no way for them even to try.

Worrying reports of potential electoral fraud were not confined to London or Pakistan but by the end of the election campaign were flooding in from all over the country.

A thirty nine year old Conservative party member had been arrested and bailed in Peterborough, (Telegraph 06/05/2010) indicating, if he was guilty, which of course has yet to be determined, a considerable degree of chutzpah given the jailing of vote riggers in Peterborough only a couple of years before.

Lancashire constabulary was investigating alleged "irregularities" in postal voting in Jack Straw's seat of Blackburn. The local council "said it was co-operating with the police investigation"

(http://news.bbc.co.uk/1/hi/uk_politics/election_2010/england/86609 66.stm)

Greater Manchester police were investigating similar allegations in the nearby areas of Oldham, Rochdale, Manchester itself and Bolton although according to press reports they related to breaches of the Electoral Code of Practice which as we have seen does not in itself have the force of law. (Telegraph 06/05/2010)

In the West Midlands Detective Inspector Mark Salt told BBC News that Birmingham was now "no worse than other cities for electoral fraud"
(http://news.bbc.co.uk/1/hi/uk_politics/election_2010/england/86493 79.stm)

Depending on one's view of other cities this could be taken as either reassurance or as damning with faint praise. In Bradford for example, police investigations were ongoing yet again as they were in Tower Hamlets, Lambeth, Barking & Dagenham, Westminster, Enfield, Hounslow, Haringey, Bexleyheath, Camden, Redbridge, Hillingdon and Bromley. Probably the official biscuit taker so far for the 2010 elections however, is the Yorkshire town of Halifax.

In April the Conservative councillor David Ginley and Conservative council candidate Mohammed Rashid were arrested on suspicion of electoral fraud. They have been bailed and at the time of writing enquiries are continuing. It is important to remember that both are completely innocent until proven guilty – there may not have been fraud or it may have taken place without the knowledge or consent of either man. The fact that Mr Ginley has previous convictions for electoral offences, in 1993 and for forgery, in 2003 does not mean he is not completely innocent now. (Election Fraud Probe Arrest, Halifax Courier, 21/04/2010)

Come polling day in Halifax and the accusations were reversed. Around four thousand postal ballots were cast, the majority being delivered by hand to polling stations. The successful Labour candidate's majority in this election was only one thousand four hundred and seventy-two.

"Local Tory officials raised concerns over the validity of some of the postal ballots after they discovered that a number of empty and derelict addresses in one particular ward had voters registered to them. They allege that Labour Party activists spent the days before the election "farming" postal ballots to deliver directly on 6 May and have asked both the police and the Electoral Commission to investigate." (Independent 26/05/2010)

The "particular ward" referred to is Park Ward, a Labour council seat with 2,283 registered postal voters.

"The Tories say they have uncovered evidence of voter impersonation, phantom registrations and voter intimidation which they have passed on to the police."   (Independent 26/05/2010)

The Halifax Evening Courier quoted Parliamentary candidate Philip Allott as saying "..it seems people were put under duress to surrender voting letters. In thirty years of politics I have never seen anything quite like this." (Courier 27/05/2010)

The election staff of Calderdale council, which covers the Halifax area say that the signatures on all postal votes were checked and there is absolutely no reason to doubt them. However, as we have seen, that is *only* a safeguard against vote riggers sending off postal votes themselves in the names of genuine voters. If postal votes have been , say, handed over to party activists, or intercepted by them on their way to the polling station, then the voting intention can be altered and the tellers have no choice but to accept that vote as valid.

If the name on the electoral register was that of a ghost voter then the signatures council staff are comparing will both be those of the vote rigger and the vote will pass.

If a voter has been bribed, tricked, persuaded or intimidated into completing their vote for a certain party or handing over a signed, blank form the vote will pass.

If the scanners are not one hundred per cent effective (and very few scanners dealing with something as erratic as human handwriting are) then false signatures will slip through and the votes will pass.

Also as Conservative Parliamentary candidate Phillip Allott says the scanners do not check if the same person's signature comes up twice or more. If there are ghost voters on the register a well organised crook could cast hundreds of votes in their names just as happened in Slough.

In addition, Liberal Democrat peer Lord Shutt of Greetland has told both the local paper and the Electoral Commission that votes were counted on election night away from central count where they could not be seen by the candidates and scrutineers. (Courier 27/05/2010)

It is illegal to do any such thing without giving the candidates and their agents forty-eight hours notice so that they can arrange to have scrutineers present. It remains to be seen whether anything will happen about this or whether, as with the ballot box seals in London's 2008 elections, vital safeguards against fraud will simply be ignored.

Unfortunately we will not get to see any of this tested in an Election Court - the only kind, remember, that can overturn an election – leaving the horrifying possibility that the police might find irrefutable evidence of widespread fraud, carried out without the knowledge or consent of the winning candidate, leaving the people of Halifax stuck with an MP they didn't vote for.

The reason is time and money. As we have seen Election Courts require a substantial financial commitment on the part of the complainants, the Election Petition must be put within 21 days of the election and the complainants must gather the evidence themselves.

"Just to raise a challenge would cost around £100, 000 –or £200, 000 if we lost" (Independent 26/05/2010) Mr Allott told reporters. Understandably, especially at the end of a hard fought election campaign, the local party just doesn't have the cash.

It is only fair to note that the Labour MP for Halifax, Linda Riordan believes the Conservative complaints are an attempt to distract attention from the arrest of two of their activists on electoral fraud charges.

"The Tory complaints are a smokescreen to divert attention away from the fact that two of their candidates have been investigated over electoral fraud allegations, " she said. "They are simply upset that they lost."

As with almost every other allegation of fraud that surfaced during this election we are, at the time of writing, in suspense. None of the police investigations have been completed, nor has the report of the Electoral Commission on the General and local elections. They do indicate however, that the *expectation* of electoral fraud has become a part of everyday political life across large parts of the country.

2010 was the first ever British General Election to be monitored by foreign observers, a development made possible by recent changes to the law. The Royal Commonwealth Society and the Commonwealth Parliamentary Association took advantage of this to send a joint team including Parliamentarians from Jamaica, Kenya, Rwanda, Nigeria, Sri Lanka, Malaysia, Bangladesh, Ghana, Guyana and Sierra Leone, a fact which some commentators clearly found embarrassing. This is unsurprising in a country that until recently prided itself on housing what was once called the "Mother of Parliaments".

It seems a shame then that on polling day, under the eyes of these distinguished visitors our arrangements in several towns and cities showed signs of falling apart.

In the seat of Wyre and Preston North a fourteen year old, Alfie McKenzie, managed to vote. It is hard to know what to be concerned about first. Mr McKenzie was entered on the electoral roll as a result of the council's own actions, sending staff round to register voters but apparently not making it clear to those they spoke to that they were gathering info for the electoral register, not the census.

The fact that Wyre and Preston North was *not* one of the seats previously mentioned as a possible site of fraud begs the question how many other names are on the register in how many other areas that shouldn't be?

In the article he wrote for the Guardian Alfie McKenzie comes across as clearly intelligent, articulate and thoughtful, a young man who actually looked at the issues, tried to inform himself politically and considered who would be best to vote for before casting his ballot.

The sneaking suspicion lingers that illegal or not he is clearly far better fitted to vote than the kind of person who hands over blank proxies. (Guardian 09/05/2010)

In polling stations across the country huge queues developed, leading to long delays. In many cases voters were turned away at 10pm after having been waiting for considerable periods. UK electoral law is very clear that "There is no provision for the extension of polling time, or for the issue of ballot papers, beyond 10pm" (Electoral Commission. "2010 UK Parliamentary general election Interim Report: Review of problems at polling stations at close of poll on 6 May 2010") Voters who have legitimately

been issued with ballots before 10pm may cast them, provided they do so without undue delay. Voters who have queued for hours but did not get issued with a ballot lose their right to vote. "No one may be issued with a ballot paper after 10pm even if they are inside the polling station and waiting to receive their ballot paper." (Interim Report)

Voters in Liverpool, Hackney, Islington, Lewisham Newcastle, Sheffield, Birmingham, Manchester, Milton Keynes and Runnymede were forced to queue for hours or actually turned away . Ironically, Runnymede was the site of the signing of Magna Carta, regarded by many as the first foundation stone of English liberties.

In Sheffield, when officials realised that there was a problem, students were placed in a different (and slower) queue from everybody else. (Guardian 07/05/2010)There can be absolutely no justification for this except on the assumption that students are somehow not "real" residents and their right to vote is less valid than that of others. The excuse given was that many students had arrived without their polling cards and this was causing undue elay. (http://news.bbc.co.uk/1/hi/uk_politics/election_2010/8666338.stm)

The excuse is pathetically flimsy. Voters turn up without polling cards at every election and as anyone who has ever worked on a polling station knows it takes mere seconds to look them up on the register.

In Liverpool there were delays when one polling station claimed to have run out of ballot papers, an excuse that borders on the surreal. Every polling station is supposed to start the day with ballot papers equivalent to the number of registered voters in the area.

In several areas, including Hackney, where a sit in was staged, and Lewisham, police were called to drive off frustrated and disenfranchised members of the public in scenes reminiscent of some impoverished emerging country where the local warlords have just staged a plebiscite

It is rare for there to be *any* significant queues at UK polling stations. Queues that last for hours and lead to hundreds of voters being turned away have not happened in living memory. How did we come to this?

Some were quick to blame increased turnout. As an explanation this has the merit of not having any merit at all. The turnout averaged around sixty-five per cent. The average turnout for UK General Elections between nineteen-sixty and nineteen-ninety-five was seventy-six per cent. (Controversies in Voting Behaviour, edited by Richard G Niemi & Herbert F. Weisberg, CQ Press 2001)

New Labour architect Peter Mandelson said "What the returning officers should have done was brought everybody in and locked the door." (Belfast Telegraph 07/05/2010)

This would, of course, have solved nothing since it would still have been unlawful to issue ballots after 10pm – proof positive that just because a politician is profoundly ignorant doesn't stop him having an opinion. To be fair to New Labour, ignorance was bipartisan – Tory Chair Eric Pickles made much the same suggestion (Belfast Telegraph 07/05/2010)

Next in line for blame was the Electoral Commission. The Mail ran an article about Commission head Jenny Watson calling her "the Modern Militant" (Mail 09/05/2010) Exactly what Ms Watson's not noticeably hardline politics had to do with anything was not clearly explained. Neither was the fact that the Electoral Commission *doesn't* run elections.

Elections are run by Returning Officers appointed by the local council, usually, but not necessarily the council's Chief Executive. What the Electoral Commission does is provide guidelines and legal advice as to how elections *should* be run (As well as writing post mortem reports into what went wrong.) The Commission cannot force Returning Officers to do anything.

Under pressure the Electoral Commission produced an interim report on the causes of voters being turned away within a fortnight. (The full report on the General Election would wait until July) It blamed the debacle on the decision by Returning Officers in many areas to assume turnouts would be low, to employ fewer staff per registered voter than the Commission had recommended and to fail to take into account the delays caused by multiple elections (In Lewisham for example voters were choosing an MP, local councillors and a directly elected mayor.)

The Commission's interim report (available on the Electoral Commission website) recommended that Returning Officers should review their staffing assumptions, that the law should be changed to allow any eligible voter present at a polling station by closing time to cast their vote and that the rules of electoral administration should be reformed to make Returning Officers more accountable. In the meantime those voters turned away have still had no redress. No election petitions were brought, probably because of the difficulties of proving the election result was changed as well as the traditional obstacles of the need to gather one's own evidence and put up financial bonds far beyond the reach of the average man or woman.

Shami Chakrabarti of the civil rights organisation "Liberty" was quoted as saying

"Anyone who feels they were denied their fundamental right to vote should contact us urgently. Liberty will use all legal and campaigning means to ensure this disgrace is never repeated." (Mail 09/05/2010)

Unfortunately there is nothing now that Liberty can do to give people their vote back – the deadline for election petitions has passed. Legal compensation might still be won for those disenfranchised but that is not the same thing at all.

The team of Commonwealth election observers were polite but deeply unimpressed.

"There has to be some doubt over the legitimacy of the result." A Sierra Leone MP told journalists. "Where people have been disenfranchised or cases of fraud are found there should be another vote. In my country this would be very controversial." (Mail 09/05/2010)

Although the observers liked " the calm and civilised way in which campaigning voting and the counting of the ballots takes place" ("Commonwealth Observer Team To The UK General Election 2010 – Final Report" pg 1 – available online at the Royal Commonwealth Society website) their final report also noted "the system itself contains vulnerabilities that make the system *corruptible* and open to fraud. The UK electoral system operates under trust; it is assumed and understood that both officials and voters are honest and do not have plans to defraud the electorate. Because of this vulnerabilities have not been addressed and may not be recognised as weaknesses in the system. Trust may have been a sufficient anchor for the system in the past, but while trust is good, caution and deterrent controls are better." (Commonwealth Observer Report pg 2)

Specifically, the report noted that "the postal voting system was divorced from the democratic process...the process does not contain mechanisms to prevent fraudulent applications for postal votes." (Commonwealth Observer Report pg 5)

The report recommended an end to postal voting on demand, wanted identification to become compulsory for voters, raised concerns over the security of the ballot boxes and called for fundamental changes to the register to put a stop to padding of rolls with ghost voters – exactly the demands reformers have been making for years. Whether the UK is mature enough to learn from its former colonies remains to be seen.

What Is To Be Done? (To Coin A Phrase)

We are living at a time when there is widespread dissatisfaction with politics and society as it is. A quick look in the politics or society section of any large bookshop will confirm that.

Shelves overflow with titles such as Taking Liberties, The Abolition of Liberty, The Abolition of Britain, The Vote: How It Was Won and How It was Undermined, Whose Side Are They On? How Big Brother Government is Ruining Britain, Time To Emigrate?, Plundering the Public Sector and many more. Yet, as I said in my preface, there is not one book on the topic of electoral fraud in Britain today with the exception of the verdict of the Birmingham election court, which Spokesman Books bound and published as "Fraud At The Elections".

In the spring of 2010 a campaign called Power 2010 was launched to press politicians for reform, including electoral reform, but the security of the vote has not even reached its top ten issues. The only mention of it I could find on the website was a suggestion that postal votes should be "tightened up".

I cannot agree. Like the Venice Commission I believe that any form of remote voting is unsafe be it postal, text or electronic. There are not, and never can be sufficient guarantees that the vote is cast and counted the way the voter intends without doing away with the secrecy of the ballot by giving a receipt showing how the vote was cast.

This would immediately lay voters open to pressure or bribery.

The best system of postal voting, that with strictly checked electoral registers and personal identifiers is *still not secret.* There is a case for a small amount of postal voting to avoid disenfranchising the sick and the infirm – it will still be used to steal votes as we saw in St Ives but as long as good reasons, endorsed by third party professionals have to be given it will only very rarely swing elections. Nor is remote e-voting secret, even if it could be safeguarded against hacking whereas to have e-voting at the polling station is simply to add an unnecessary layer of obfuscation, expense and opportunity for error or fraud.

 E-counting is open to manipulation, error and a total lack of transparency. It is an example of what Americans call black box voting, where there is no true way for ordinary people to be sure their voting is free and fair. Ironically, when it comes to elections low tech solutions, paper ballots, sealed metal boxes, marked registers, supervised polling places etc are more secure than anything else the best brains can come up with. This is not a Luddite view, it is one that the IT specialists of the Open Rights Group largely share. It is a view the Electoral Commission has moved some way towards since the heady days when they spoke excitedly of e-enabled General Elections.

We have had, only just over a year ago a General Election in this country. It took place under the same rules that failed to stop the frauds in Slough, that Mawrey calculated would have only stopped one out of fourteen methods of fraud at Birmingham. Anyone trying to overturn the election of any MP would have been faced with a colossal task of fund raising and organisation. Like Salma Yaqoob in 2005 they would most likely have found it impossible to get legal aid. We can only hope the 2010 election was free and fair, but as the rapporteurs for the Council of Europe concluded, if it was, it was despite our electoral system not because of it.

In the United States and the Netherlands campaigns for better vote security have had a measure of success and a considerable impact on public opinion. Despite the fact that public confidence in the UK voting system is among the lowest in Western Europe there has been no such success here. This is not because no one has tried.

Individuals such as John Hemming MP, groups such as Unlock Democracy, Stamp Out Voting Fraud, the Open Rights Group, noted journalists and even, at times, the Electoral Commission have tried to make us aware, to rouse public opinion.

It is our own fault if we have failed to listen.

I would urge anyone who reads this book and finds the topic urgent, who believes that what is going on is wrong, to make their public mark.

Go to your union and put a motion opposing postal votes on demand, demanding that unsealed ballot boxes be set aside for criminal investigation, not simply counted, that e-counting be stopped, that election petitions be reformed so that it doesn't take a fortune to challenge a stolen vote.

Write to your MP demanding the same. Take it up with your political party if you are a member of one. Point out again and again that however small the scandals we have had may seem to some, they expose a gaping wound at the core of our democracy and if matters are left unchecked the lifeblood of our democracy can pour out of them.

Many years ago, Ignazio Silone, a man who had seen democratic Italy succumb to Fascism and fled his native land asked "Has a servile people ever remained free for long?" (The School For Dictators)

While we tolerate elections where votes are stolen, postmen robbed of ballot envelopes, voters pressured or threatened, where counts are impossible to verify, where ballot boxes are brought in with the seals hanging open, where non-existent people vote in their hundreds, where only the wealthy or the party machines can hope to bring election petitions and where thousands of ballots emerge from boxes that only hundreds were counted going into we are a servile people and our freedom hangs in the balance.

Bibliography and Sources

Books

Atkins, Chris *Taking Liberties* London; Revolver Books 2007

Benyon, John & Solomos, John (Ed) *The Roots of Urban Unrest* Oxford; Pergamon Press 1987

Carvel, John *Turn Again Livingstone* London; Profile Books 1999

Craig, David & Brooks, Richard *Plundering the Public Sector* London; Constable 2006

Evans, Maya & Rai, Milan *Naming The Dead: A Serious Crime* London; Drava Papers 2006

Flynn, Paul *Dragons Led By Poodles: The Inside Story of A New Labour Stitch-up* London; Politico's Publishing 1999

Foot, Paul *The Vote: How It Was Won, and How It Was Undermined* London; Viking 2005

Gilmour, Ian *Riots, Risings and Revolution* London; Hutchinson 1992

Gumbel, Andrew *Steal This Vote: Dirty Elections and the Rotten History of Democracy In America* New York; Nation Books 2005

Hain, Peter *The Democratic Alternative: A Socialist response to Britain's Crisis* London; Penguin Books Ltd 1983

Harris, Robert *The Making of Neil Kinnock* London; Faber & Faber 1984

Hattersley, Roy *Who Goes Home? Scenes From A Political Life* London; Little Brown and Company 1995

Hollingsworth, Mark *The Press And Political Dissent* London; Pluto Press 1986

Holt , Tom *Alexander At The World's End* London; Abacus Books 2000

Kaufman, Gerald (Ed) *The Left: A Symposium* London; Anthony Blond 1966

King, Oona *House Music: The Oona King Diaries* London; Bloomsbury Publishing Plc 2008

Littlejohn Richard *Littlejohn's Britain* London; Arrow 2007

Long, James *Game Ten* London; Pocket Books 1995

Mawrey, Richard *Fraud At The Elections: The Final and Definitive Judgement of Election Commissioner Richard Mawrey QC Handed Down On Monday 4th April 2005 In The Matters of Local Government Elections For The Bordesley Green And Aston Wards Of The Birmingham City Council Both Held On 10th June 2004* Nottingham; Spokesman Books 2005

Mortimer, John *Rumpole and the Golden Thread* London; Penguin Books 1983

Moss, Robert *The Collapse of Democracy* London; Sphere Books 1977

Niemi, Richard G. & Weisberg Herbert F. *Controversies in Voting Behaviour* New York CQ Press 1993

Pearce, Alan *Whose Side Are They On?* London; Gibson Square Books Ltd 2009

Plowden, Alison *The Case of Eliza Armstrong* London; BBC 1974

Rogers, PG *Battle in Bossenden Wood: The Strange Story of Sir William Courtenay* Oxford; Readers Union, Oxford University Press 1962

Rose, David *In The Name of the Law: The Collapse of Criminal Justice* London; Vintage 1996

Silone, Ignazio *The School For Dictators* London; Johnathan Cape 1939

Steel, Mark *Reasons To Be Cheerful* London; Scribner 2002

Online Resources

BBC News 06/12/2002 *Councillors Jailed for vote rigging*
http://news.bbc.co.uk/1/hi/england/2551157.stm

BBC News 01/05/2010 *Chasing the UK vote in Pakistan's 'Little Britain'*
(http://news.bbc.co.uk/1/hi/uk_politics/election_2010/8655697.stm

BBC News 04/05/2010 *Inquiry into Blackburn postal vote 'irregularity'*
(http://news.bbc.co.uk/1/hi/uk_politics/election_2010/england/86609
66.stm)

BBC News *Birmingham postal voting 'is now safer'*
http://news.bbc.co.uk/1/hi/uk_politics/election_2010/england/8649379.st
m

BBC News *Inquiry as voters miss out as polls shut*
http://news.bbc.co.uk/1/hi/uk_politics/election_2010/8666338.stm

Channel 4 News *Vote Rigging Claims Raise Electoral Questions*
(http://www.channel4.com/news/articles/uk/vote+rigging+claims+rai
se+electoral+questions/3636102)

Joseph Rowntree Reform Trust *Purity of Elections In the UK: Causes
for Concern*
http://www.jrrt.org.uk/uploads/Purity%20of%20Elections%20in%20the%
20UK%20-%20Executive%20Summary.pdf

Parliamentary Committee on Standards in Public Life *Restoring Integrity
to the Electoral System* http://www.public-
standards.gov.uk/OurWork/Restoring_integrity_to_the_Electoral_System
.html

John Borras, Director, Technology Policy, Office of the e-Envoy Cabinet
Office *eVoting:Standards for UK Elections*
http://xml.coverpages.org/BorrasUK-Evoting.pdf

Electoral Commission report *Securing The Vote*
http://www.electoralcommission.org.uk/__data/assets/pdf_file/0006/4717
5/Securingthevote_17643-12944__E__N__S__W__.pdf

Electoral Commission report *Delivering Democracy ? The Future of
Postal Voting*
http://www.electoralcommission.org.uk/__data/assets/electoral_commiss

ion_pdf_file/0015/13164/DeliveringDemocracyfinalcomplete_16306-10935__E__N__S__W__.pdf

Electoral Commission report *Voting for Change: An electoral law modernisation programme*
http://www.electoralcommission.org.uk/__data/assets/electoral_commiss
ion_pdf_file/0017/16055/Votingforchange_16305-
7978_E_N_S_W_.pdf

Electoral Commission report *Electoral Pilot Scheme Evaluation Rushmoor Borough Council*
http://www.electoralcommission.org.uk/__data/assets/electoral_commiss
ion_pdf_file/0013/13180/Rushmoor_22977-
17164_E_N_S_W_.pdf

Electoral Commission report *The 2004 European Elections in the UK*
http://www.electoralcommission.org.uk/__data/assets/electoral_commiss
ion_pdf_file/0018/13167/ECPartElections2004_15438-
11422_E_N_S_W_.pdf

Electoral Commission report *The Greater London Authority Elections 2008: Report on the administration of the 1 May 2008 elections*
http://www.electoralcommission.org.uk/__data/assets/pdf_file/0005/5785
7/GLA-Elections-Report-2008-revised.pdf

Joint Electoral Commission and ACPO report *Allegations of electoral malpractice at the May 2008 elections in England and Wales*
http://www.electoralcommission.org.uk/__data/assets/pdf_file/0005/7458
8/Allegations-of-Electoral-Malpractice-Web-Final.pdf

Electoral Commission report *2010 UK Parliamentary General Election Interim Report: review of problems at polling stations at close of poll on 6th May 2010*
http://www.electoralcommission.org.uk/__data/assets/pdf_file/0010/9909
1/Interim-Report-Polling-Station-Queues-complete.pdf

Electoral Commission report *Report on the administration of the 2010 General Election*
http://www.electoralcommission.org.uk/__data/assets/pdf_file/0010/1007
02/Report-on-the-administration-of-the-2010-UK-general-election.pdf

Electoral Commission Report *The Glenrothes UK Parliamentary by-election; report on the administration of the 6th November 2008 by-election*
http://www.electoralcommission.org.uk/__data/assets/pdf_file/0016/7213
3/Glenrothes-final-with-cover3-web.pdf

The Gould Report, commissioned by the Electoral Commission *Scottish Elections 2007 The independent review of the Scottish Parliamentary and local government elections 3 May 2007*
http://www.electoralcommission.org.uk/__data/assets/electoral_commiss
ion_pdf_file/0011/13223/Scottish-Election-Report-A-Final-For-Web.pdf

Scottish Courts Services Report *Investigation into Missing Electoral Register*
www.scots.courts.gov.uk/docs/report/Report_Investigation_Into_Missing
_Electoral_Register2009.pdf

High Court Election Petition Simmons v Khan
http://www.slough.info/law/law41/law41.html

Select Committee on Home Affairs 1998: Fourth Report: Electoral Law and Administration http://www.parliament.the-stationery-office.co.uk/pa/cm199798/cmselect/cmhaff/768/76803.htm

Craig Murray blog archive *"Jack Straw Should Be In Jail"*
http://www.craigmurray.org.uk/archives/2007/06/jack_straw_shou_1/

Craig Murray blog *"Jack Thwarted"*
(http://www.craigmurray.org.uk/archives/2010/05/jack_thwarted)

Parliamentary Committee on Standards in Public Life Press Release 18 March 2008
http://www.egenda.stockton.gov.uk/aksstockton/images/att5479.pdf

Official notes to the Political Parties, Elections and Referendums Act 2000 http://www.legislation.gov.uk/ukpga/2000/41/notes/contents

The Election Petition (Amendment) Rules 2003
http://www.legislation.gov.uk/uksi/2003/972/contents/made

Digital Voting and Fraternal Rights, Bob Watt, University of Essex, Department of Law http://www.nesc.ac.uk/talks/639/16-

15%20Bob%20Watt%20mon%20afternoon%20digital%20voting%20and
%20fraternal%20rights.pdf

Metropolitan Police Authority report: *Electoral Offences in London
following the local elections of May 2006*
*http://www.mpa.gov.uk/committees/mpa/2006/061026/14/?qu=Electoral
%20fraud&sc=2&ht=1*

Venice Commission report on the compatibility of remote voting withthe
standards of the Council of Europe
http://www.venice.coe.int/docs/2004/CDL-AD(2004)012-e.asp

The Open Rights Group May 2007 Election Report
http://www.openrightsgroup.org/campaigns/e-voting/e-voting-2007/e-
voting-main

The Open Rights Group May 2008 Election Report
http://www.openrightsgroup.org/wp-
content/uploads/orglondonelectionsreport.pdf

"We Do Not Trust Voting Machines"
http://wijvertrouwenstemcomputersniet.nl/English

CESG Report on eVoting Security – Response of the Centre for
Computing and Social Responsibility, De Montfort University
http://www.ccsr.cse.dmu.ac.uk/resources/general/responses/evoting-
security.html

The Association of Electoral Administrators *Counting Arrangements for
the General Election – an AEA Issues Paper* *http://www.aea-
elections.co.uk/downloads/friday_count_issues_paper.pdf*

The Electoral Administration Act & Explanatory Notes
http://www.legislation.gov.uk/ukpga/2006/22/notes/contents

Council of Europe Parliamentary Assembly *Application to initiate a
monitoring procedure to investigate electoral fraud in the United
Kingdom*
http://www.assembly.coe.int/CommitteeDocs/2008/electoral_fraud_UK_
E.pdf

House of Commons Library Research Briefing *Postal Voting and Electoral Fraud*
http://www.parliament.uk/documents/commons/lib/research/briefings/snp c-03667.pdf

Official explanatory notes to the Political Parties and Elections Act 2009
http://www.legislation.gov.uk/ukpga/2009/12/pdfs/ukpgaen_20090012_e n.pdf

Actica Consulting *An assessment of the procurement and management of the electronic counting system used at the 2008 GLA elections*
http://www.electoralcommission.org.uk/__data/assets/pdf_file/0009/5906 7/Acticas-report-on-the-management-and-procurement-of-the-2008-GLA-elections.pdf

The Royal Commonwealth Society & The Commonwealth Parliamentary Association, UK Branch Commonwealth Observer Team to the UK General Election 2010 Final Report

http://www.thercs.org/society/Filestore/PDFDownloads/Commonwealth_Election_Observers_Final_Report.pdf

http://stolenvotes.org.uk

Newspapers and Magazines, in order cited

Guardian 14/01/2010

Newcastle Journal 13/01/2010

Morning Star 29/04/2008

Guardian 09/05/2001

Lancashire Telegraph 08/02/2008

Guardian 03/06/2005

Birmingham Mail 08/06/2004

Telegraph 14/04/2005

Guardian 11/04/2005

Guardian 15/04/2005

Telegraph 22/03/2004

Times 23/02/2005

Independent on Sunday 10/04/2005

Times 10/04/2005

Telegraph 06/05/2005

Bradford Telegraph and Argus 07/09/2010

Guardian 03/06/2005

Times 26/03/2005

Reading Evening Post 23/03/2005

Evening Standard 03/05/2005

Socialist Review May 2005

Mail 06/04/2005

Socialist Worker 13/11/1999

Independent 28/10/1999

Guardian 04/11/1999

Guardian 18/04/2009

Tribune 20/04/2009

Guardian 25/04/2009

Telegraph 15/04/2009

Guardian 18/04/2009

Telegraph 18/04/2009

Guardian 29/09/2010

Time Magazine 03/11/2007

Guardian 22/11/2008

Socialist Renewal 02/01/2007

The Glenrothes Courier 06/03/2009

Guardian 08/04/2010

Evening Standard 30/04/2010

Derby Telegraph 28/04/2010

Mail 04/05/2010

Independent 04/05/2010

Times 09/05/2010

Telegraph 06/05/2010

Halifax Courier 21/04/2010

Independent 26/05/2010

Halifax Courier 27/05/2010

Guardian 09/05/2010

Guardian 07/05/2010

Belfast Telegraph 07/05/2010

Mail 09/05/2010